OUT OF THE WILDERNESS
A history of
SITKA
MICHIGAN

SUSAN ZERLAUT KING

Published in Hackham Australia
February 2025 by
Immortalise
P. O. Box 656
Noarlunga Centre SA 5163
Australia

ISBN 978-1-7637149-8-4

Copyright © Susan Zerlaut King 2018, 2025.

All rights reserved. Other than for the purposes and subject to the conditions prescribed under the *Copyright Act*, no part of this publication may be reproduced, stored in a retrieval system, or transmitted in any form or by any means, electronic, mechanical, photocopying, recording or otherwise, without the prior permission of the publisher.

Cataloguing-in-Publication entry is available from the National Library of Australia http:/catalogue.nla.gov.au/.

First edition published in 2018, this edition published in 2025.

Typesetting by John Healy, 2025 modifications by Ben Morton.

In memory of
Herman Walter Zerlaut
(1922-2011)

whose valuable Zerlaut family
research from Germany to America
sparked my curiosity about our
family

and

Mabel (Wheaton) Ruggles
(1885-1966)

whose dedication to reporting
the Sitka community news
for nearly 50 years
brought Sitka to life for me.

Contents

Author's Note 7

Introduction 9

Chapter One
The Wilderness 11

Chapter Two
The Treaty Years and Statehood 20

Chapter Three
Treaties and Tragedy 23

Chapter Four
The Boom 28

Chapter Five
The Civil War 34

Chapter Six
Moving Forward 44

Chapter Seven
Sitka and the Alaska Purchase 48

Chapter Eight
Educating the Young 49

Chapter Nine
The Invisible Enemy 52

Chapter Ten
A Town in the Making 60

Chapter Eleven
Bands and Baseball 64

Chapter Twelve
Sitka Grange Hall No. 861 67

Chapter Thirteen
The Little Church with the Big Heart 72

Chapter Fourteen
Supporting Organizations of the Church 77

Chapter Fifteen
  Rallies, Revivals, and Temperance 82

Photo Section 85

Chapter Sixteen
  The Church and the Schools 103

Chapter Seventeen
  Pandemic and War 107

Chapter Eighteen
  Tragedies 114

Chapter Nineteen
  Roaring Twenties and the Great Depression 124

Chapter Twenty
  Orchards Come to Sitka 127

Chapter Twenty-one
  War Again 132

Chapter Twenty-two
  The Labor Shortage 142

Chapter Twenty-three
  Those Who Served—World War II 147

Chapter Twenty-four
  The Post-War Years 154

Chapter Twenty-five
  The Milk Withholding Action 161

Chapter Twenty-six
  Sitka Today 166

Epilogue 168

Appendices 171
  Teachers of Kempf School 171
  Students of Kempf School (1901-1902) 173
  Students of Kempf School (1911-1912) 174
  Students of Kempf School (1924-1925) 175
  Teachers of Jibson School 176

Students of Jibson School (1901-1902) 178
Students of Jibson School (1911-1912) 179
Students of Jibson School (1924-1925) 180
Sitka Methodist Episcopal Church
Subscription Document of 1908 181
Members of the Ladies Aid Society 1908 183

Bibliography 184

Author's Note

Though this book will mainly center on the community of Sitka, Michigan, this story cannot be told without understanding the history that preceded it. The importance of the surrounding areas, who came, who stayed, and why, is necessary in showing the development of the community.

Many families were part of the making of Sitka. Some of them I know and had a lot of information about them; others very little. I have made every effort to include as many families and individuals as I could. I've strived to keep to the facts as I understand them and let the reader know when something is merely speculation. To this end I hope this book will honor all those who came before us.

Many thanks to all those who provided information, photos, family histories, read drafts, and who gave encouragement when it seemed I would never finish. This is your story, too.

Susan Zerlaut King

Introduction

Several years ago I became interested in my ancestors, the family of both my mother, Grace Emma Abbott, and my father, Harold Willius Zerlaut. Though I have extensively researched both families, this writing focuses on my father's family and the small community into which he was born in 1899, and lived in for 92 years. This is the community of Sitka, which lies on the border between Sheridan and Bridgeton townships, in the county of Newaygo, Michigan.

As I dutifully filled in the lines of my family tree with all those names and dates of births, marriages, and deaths, I couldn't help wondering about the people whose information I was recording. These people, my family, were more than a compilation of dates. They must have had hopes and dreams, hardships, sicknesses, ordinary experiences and sometimes extraordinary ones, and maybe even just plain fun.

I couldn't get these people out of my head. I sorted through boxes of photos my parents had saved and thankfully labeled. Among the family photos were old photos of Sitka. There was the Methodist church, newly built in 1908; across the road was the Grange hall with all those tall windows. The general store had wagons with horses pulled up front. There was, as well, a blacksmith shop and even a post office. Clearly, this had been a thriving community in the early 1900s.

To learn more about Sitka I decided to check out the historical library in Fremont. After some initial investigation, I began to read the old Fremont Times Indicator on microfilm. What I thought would be a couple hours of mildly interesting reading had me hooked when I realized Sitka had a community news correspondent dating as far back as 1912. I remembered the Sitka community news from when I was growing up in the 1950s and 60s. It informed people of activities in and around Sitka.

All the little communities in the area contributed their news to the paper. I have to admit, back then it all seemed pretty boring. But to know what people thought and did way back in 1912—well, that caught my interest.

A couple hours became two years. I read through the years from 1912 to the mid-1950s and, like a giant puzzle, the pieces of Sitka slowly came together to reveal an active, close-knit community. These were people who looked out for each other during hard times, worked to improve their community, and always strived to learn—and they had a real passion for life. This is their story, as best I can tell it, with a little help from my ancestors.

Susan Zerlaut King

Chapter One

The Wilderness

A person making an unexpected journey down rural Dickinson Ave—probably having made a wrong turn and searching for some kind of main road—comes unexpectedly to a crossroads with a ghost town appearance. To one side sits an old stone church with large stained glass windows. Etched into one of the stones is the date of 1908. Nearby a gray-weathered town hall building has the weary look of many years' disuse. A very large, gnarled oak tree with considerable lightning damage leans precariously.

Across from the church a deserted, shuttered farm house and barn immersed in tall weeds and grass is surrounded by dying fruit trees. An old family cemetery sits off to the side in a nearby field. Running alongside the farm house a road with a rusty sign warns: 'Road Closed'.

With puzzlement the traveler looks at the church sign once more. Sitka? Where the heck am I?

* * *

I am a child of Sitka. Born in 1946, I have a very different view of Sitka than my imagined traveler, as did my parents, grandparents, great-grandparents, and great-great-grandmother. If we could go back in time before the middle of the 1800s the view would be even more drastically altered.

As a child I spent many hours playing outside on our family farm, wandering through the gullies, climbing trees, wading in Brooks Creek, often pretending to live in 'Indian' times. Though I'm sure I had some interesting imaginations, never could I have pictured what my home was really like before Michigan statehood. The forests had been full of millions of pines, their tops stretching two hundred feet into the sky. These same forests and waters were teeming with fur-bearing animals; beaver, martin, and muskrat. The rivers and lakes were filled with large quantities of fish; lake sturgeon, Artic grayling, and numerous water fowl. There were no buildings—except for the few coverings the Indians constructed—or roads other than the trails of Indians, those left by deer, or other large animals. In fact, to even walk through this wilderness was extremely difficult because of the denseness of the forest packed tightly together with hundreds of years' growth.

In winter the trees and brush were buried with heavy snow, making travel even more difficult. The rivers, lakes, and streams were covered with thick layers of ice. The bitter cold drove migratory birds to the south and small animals to shelter deep in the ground or in logs and trees. There was a stillness foreign to most humans today; just the sound of the cold wind through the pines and the occasional call of an eagle.

Spring brought forth flowers. The woods and clearings held Jack-in-the-pulpit or Indian turnip, the white petals of trillium, graceful columbine, colorful lupines, pink lady slippers or moccasin flower, and flowering dogwood. The bees would quickly begin the process of making honey. Black bear would emerge from winter rest to start the process of assuaging their ravenous appetites and those of their cubs. They would feed on the new green vegetation, insects, and the fruit of the wild strawberry and blueberry. Soon the winter birds would shake off the cold as the migrating birds returned. Nesting would begin in earnest with birds calling across the treetops.

It all sounds beautiful, but for humans, this wilderness beauty had its downside. To live in the elements—to find food, shelter, and warmth—took courage, determination, and skill. There were those individuals who called this land home. They were tribes of Algonquin Indians known as the Ojibwa (Chippewa), Ottawa, and the Potawatomi.

About two hundred and thirty years before the first land patents were given in Michigan, a French explorer named Etienne Brule arrived in Quebec. He was a servant of Samuel de Champlain. In 1610 he was sent to the Algonquin Indians to learn their language and customs, and to earn their trust in order to be an interpreter for trading. His journeys took him from the shores of Lake Huron to the great falls of what would become known as Sault Ste. Marie. He explored areas around Lake Superior, Lake Ontario, Lake Erie, and possibly Lake Michigan. His explorations and trading allowed the introduction of the white man's ways into the region. Whether for good or bad, many more people followed bringing enormous changes to the people and the land of the Great Lakes.

The location of Michigan with its waterways and abundant supply of furs—beaver, bear, martin, raccoon, lynx, wolf, and fox—was perfect for the booming fur trading business. The forests abounded with fur traders. Many fur trading posts were set up to receive the merchandise. In 1790 Joseph LaFramboise was given the entire area of western Michigan as his fur trading territory. He established twenty trading posts, one being on the mouth of Duck Lake, located along Lake Michigan in Muskegon County. Joseph and his wife, Magdelaine, had a regular trading cycle. They began in the fall by trading for furs with the Indians, then returning with the furs to Mackinac Island each spring.

In 1806, while stopping for the night along the Lake Michigan shore near the mouth of the Muskegon River, Joseph refused liquor to a Potawatomi named Nequat. He was subsequently stabbed while kneeling in prayer. After his murder, Magdelaine became one of the most successful fur traders in the Northwest Territory by obtaining her own fur trading license—quite a remarkable achievement in a male-dominated business.

Magdelaine was born to a French fur trader and an Odawa mother. She spoke four languages: Ottawa, French, English, and Chippewa. Her knowledge of languages, her Native American heritage, and her business skills enabled her to thrive. At a time when most fur traders were making

$1000 per year, she was earning as much as $5000-$10,000. Magdelaine started out as an independent fur trader, but in 1818 she began working for John Jacob Astor and his American fur trading monopoly. After fifteen years in the business she retired in 1821 to Mackinac Island where she taught herself to read and write. She also helped build a school for the island's children, and established a life of philanthropy, which she pursued until her death in 1846.

As for John Jacob Astor, his role in stripping the Michigan forests of its fur-bearing animals forever changed the animal landscape our ancestors would soon settle and had enormous consequences. Many animals could no longer replenish themselves. In 1808 he established the American Fur Company. He designed a plan to buy furs in Michigan, the heart of the fur trade, and transport them back to New York in order to ship them to China in trade for tea.

Fur traders were encouraged to live with the Indians and earn their trust, thus the supply was easily met. It is unfortunate that in order to get a good trade with the Indians John Astor succumbed to supplying liquor for pelts. He eventually joined in the opium-smuggling trade as well. In 1822 Astor had established his fur company headquarters at Mackinac Island, but by the 1830s, the taste for furs was beginning to change and animals were scarce, leading Astor to quit the fur trading business in 1834 and seek other ventures. He died in 1848 having a net worth equivalent to $110.1 billion in today's money.

Other notable fur traders were active in this area during the early 1800s. They included a Frenchman named Lamarandier, who opened a trading post on the north side of the Muskegon River; another Frenchman, Jean Recollet, who started his fur trading business on Muskegon Lake in 1812; and Joseph Bailly, who traded extensively with the Ottawa at his post on Muskegon Lake and Muskegon River from 1793-1822; and his successor, Lewis B. Baddeau, whose trading post in 1834 was also located on Muskegon Lake. But the most colorful and best known of the fur traders in the area that would become Sitka was Joseph Troutier.

Chapter One: The Wilderness

* * *

Joseph Troutier (also known as 'Truckee') was born on Mackinac Island on August 9, 1812 to a French Canadian father, a fur trader, and an Ottawa Indian mother. In 1835, when Joseph was only 23 years old, he had worked his way to the Muskegon area. There he set up a trading post and post office on Muskegon Lake. He worked this post for three years before moving up the Muskegon River about 15 miles to a place called Maple Island, now part of Bridgeton Township.

The island, in the middle of the Muskegon River, was one mile wide and about two miles long. At that time the Indian trails along the river were the only means of travel. There was a considerable Indian village located nearby on what is now called Troutier or Truckee Lake. There he built his fur trading post by erecting a rough-hewn log building, about 26 x 15 feet in size. This is where Indians brought maple sugar and furs to trade. The post was also used by white settlers who eventually came, many following the lumber business, to get their supplies.

Also having a post very near Truckee, as most came to call him, was a half French, half Ottawa Indian named William Washa, also known as Indian Bill. He, too, bartered in furs and maple sugar. However, alcohol became part of the bartering process. It caused him many problems in his life, as it did for many other Indians.

Nearby, Buckhorn Dan McPhelan, another trapper and fisherman of the day, took up residence in section 20. In his later life he was paid a dollar a day by a local hotel to spend summers in Petoskey. His job was to spend time conversing with the tourists. Instead of using his earnings for transportation, McPhelan preferred to walk to and from Petoskey each summer. He died at Maple Island in 1914.

As for Truckee, he married an Indian woman who unfortunately did not live long. His second wife was another Indian woman, possibly Indian Bill's daughter. It is said that Truckee paid Indian Bill $300 for the marriage. Part of the agreement was that she would live in a wigwam behind the trading post where she cooked and slept. She wanted no part of living inside a building. She also did not live long. Truckee married a third time, again an Indian woman. It appears she was killed by a street car in Muskegon. His fourth marriage was to a woman 30 years his junior.

Though Truckee seemed unlucky in marriage, he did well in other areas of his life. He was the sort of person who did not miss an opportunity to make money. His trading post was also used as an inn. Truckee had never learned to read or write, but that did not stop him from creative accounting practices. He designed a series of pictures to help him keep track of what was owed. For those who stayed at the 'inn' and had meals he would draw a knife and fork to indicate meals that needed to be added to the bill. He also had pictures for all the supplies he sold. For instance, cheese was represented by a circle. When the bill was paid he showed the account closed by drawing a line through the picture. This method worked for him his entire life, though his inability to read and write did cause confusion at times. He once was looking at a newspaper and telling friends about a terrible storm and ship that was lost on Lake Michigan. It was later determined he was looking at a ship on Lake Michigan alright, but he had the newspaper upside down.

Another way of procuring money was Truckee's ferry system. Near his trading post was the only place for many miles where a person could easily cross the Muskegon River. He had a horse he called George which he trained to take people across the river. The horse would carry the passenger across, the rider would dismount, then George would return back to the other side of the river.

Truckee took over Isaac Merrill's trading post at Sand Creek, which runs into Sand Lake in Ashland Township, in 1869. He also had other posts, including one on the White River. All these businesses made Truckee a wealthy man for his time. He was considered honest and trustworthy, though he liked to embellish his wealth occasionally. Famously, he bragged that he had thousands of dollars in gold slugs buried on Maple Island, a claim which has led to numerous searches by treasure hunters over the years. Even his father-in-law believed this to be true and dismantled his house after he died, looking for gold. None has ever been found.

Truckee lived to be 68 years old. He died in Bridgeton on July 17, 1880 of gangrene. He was a Catholic and given last rights by an Indian priest. The Native priest held a celebration of life which was attended by a multitude of Indians and white traders and settlers. Exactly where he is buried is unknown. There are several burial sites in and around the Maple Island area and it has been assumed by many that he was buried on the island itself. There is an old Indian burial site on the north side of the river, in section 20, which is also called the Storms cemetery. No sign of graves now remain, but Sabrina Storms and other family members who lived on the property during that time told stories of Indian's howling cries as they came down the river in their canoes bringing the dead to the burial grounds. Perhaps this is where the half-Indian Joseph Troutier found his final resting place.

* * *

During the fur trading time there were very few permanent European residents. Most came, got what they wanted, and left. Those that did stay were often part Native American and took Native America women for wives. There were also the Jesuits. They followed the fur traders, making it easier for them to trade with the Indians by earning their trust. The fur trading posts, in return, made it easier for the Jesuits to come and promote salvation to the Indians.

The best-known Jesuit who worked in this area was the missionary and explorer Father Jacques Marquette. A memorial for Father Marquette still stands at the site of his death along the shore of what is now known as Ludington. In 1675, while returning from an exploratory trip to the

Mississippi to his mission in St. Ignace, he died from a bout of dysentery. He was buried near the shore temporarily and moved to St. Ignace in 1677. (Cf. Ethelyn Abbot, Michigan History Stories, 1947)

It was common for the Jesuits to give double-barred crosses, called the Cross of Lorraine, to faithful Indian chiefs and other significant Indians. It is said this cross helped convert the natives they encountered because it resembled local native imagery. Such a cross was found on Maple Island in the early 1900s. A man named P. G. Cooley bought the land formerly belonging to lumber baron Martin Ryerson on Maple Island, known as Ryerson Hills Farm. While plowing in front of one of the barns he unearthed what appeared to be a body. He called a prosecutor, Mr. Branstrom, to report a suspected murder. As you can guess the prosecutor lost no time in getting out to the farm. Mr. Branstrom dug away in the sandy soil, finally exposing a mostly intact skeleton. Upon the skeleton's chest was a double-barred cross. It appeared that it had been worn around the neck of the individual. The cross was made of copper, about five and one half inches long, with two cross-bars, the lower one thee inches long and the upper one two and three quarters long. It was greatly oxidized and appeared very old. Further digging produced many more bones and it was finally decided that Mr. Cooley had accidently plowed into an old Indian burial ground. The cross had most likely been handed down, generation to generation, and may have originally started out in other parts of Michigan. It could possibly have originated with Father Marquette himself. Also, one wonders if the skeleton unearthed was that of the Indian priest who presided over Truckee's funeral.

* * *

If the fur traders opened the door a crack to the Europeans, the beginning of the treaty years, along with the building of the Erie Canal, swung those doors wide open. Before there were steam ships and railroads most goods had to be transported by pack animals. The Erie Canal was built to create a navigable route to the Great Lakes. Construction began in 1817 and the canal was finished and opened October 26, 1825. The allure of Michigan was every adventurer's and speculator's dream. Now all those furs, timber, and minerals were so much more accessible. Prospectors came in droves to take all that was above or below ground. Nothing seemed off limits.

Chapter Two

The Treaty Years and Statehood

Western Michigan was home to three Native American tribes. Together they formed the Council of Three Fires. To the north were the Ojibwa—also called Chipppewa—the oldest of the tribes. They referred to themselves as the Anishinabe, or Original Man. The Ojibwa were hunters and fishers and moved about as necessary. They were superb canoe makers, using white cedar for the frames and birch bark for the covering. This made the canoes light enough for easy portage as they traveled the waterways.

The Potawatomi, known as the People of a Place of Fire, (or Fire Keepers) made their home mostly south of the Grand River. The Potawatomi were more settled; agricultural in nature, gardeners and growers of corn and harvesters of wild rice. The corn was ground into meal and used for hominy or made into Indian fry bread. The wild rice (minumin) was gathered in late August. The Indians would canoe into marshes containing stands of wild rice. There they gathered together stalks of rice, bundled them, then bent the tops over their canoes and beat the grains off the stalks into the bottom of their canoes. These staples were traded with other tribes and also became the stores they lived on during the winter months.

In the middle of these two tribes lived the Ottawa, known as 'The Traders'. They traded amongst themselves and with the Ojibwa and the Potawatomi. The Ottawa were also hunters and fishers. In the summer and fall they would group together along lakes and streams to pursue fishing. In those days, lake sturgeon weighing up to one hundred pounds could be easily speared from shore. Many other species of fish could be found in the waters of Lake Michigan or in nearby rivers. The Artic grayling from the salmon family was commonly found in the Muskegon River. In late August ricing would begin and then came fall trapping season. Snares were set to collect pelts for trading. There was hunting for winter food. By then fruits, berries and plants for medicinal use had been gathered and dried. It was then time for the Ottawa to move to their winter camps.

In the spring they relocated to stands of maple trees to collect sap which they collected in birch bark bowls. Maple syrup was not only a staple of their diet, but was very important in the business of trading. In fact, the area later known as Sitka was originally called Sugar Bush due to the abundance of maple trees. When I grew up in Sitka the landscape was still embraced by numerous maple trees. To walk down Dickinson Ave in the fall was to travel through a colorful tunnel of yellows, oranges, and reds tinged with green.

As a young man, my father used to plow this area with horses. He frequently unearthed arrowheads which he saved. This collection is now one of my most treasured possessions. Holding these arrowheads in my hand, it is easy for me to picture the Ottawa gathered among the maple trees collecting spring sap and making sugar.

Lloyd Jibson, a descendent of Robert Jibson, could still see evidence of the Indians tapping trees when he was young. His son Bill continues the tradition and taps the maple trees on the ancestral farm each year.

This cycle of living by nature and what the seasons provided had gone on for hundreds of years. The Native Americans respected what was given to them and did not take more than could be used. No part of an animal was discarded. All parts served some purpose. Trees and plants were only harvested to meet the needs of shelter and food. How all this could change so dramatically in such a short time span boggles the mind.

But change it did with the arrival of lumbermen and settlers. The thought of taking no more than could be replenished by nature was disregarded by many. By the end of the lumbering period the area must have looked like a wasteland to the Native Americans still remaining. As far as the eye could see there was nothing but stumps. Gone were the Artic grayling whose fish beds were destroyed by the logs rammed into their habitat during the spring thaw. The wild rice had been ripped out by dredging to make the waterways deeper for floating logs. Animal and fish populations had been diminished by over-hunting, trapping, and fishing. Trees for shelter and canoe building were difficult to find. Even though the main lumbering was pine, other trees were wrecked in the process. Medicinal plants were destroyed by rolling logs down the hillsides to the river below. The cycle of nature that Indians lived by had been demolished, never to be returned to its fullness again.

Chapter Three

Treaties and Tragedy

It is important to note that Native Americans did not understand the written word. They relied upon the spoken word so they were often misled by what the papers they signed really meant. Ownership of land was foreign to them. In their culture all was shared, so in that respect they often signed papers thinking they were sharing the land with whites. Or they signed thinking they were just selling the timber, but they were really selling the land as well. Later, many treaty agreements were simply ignored by governments and settlers in their thirst for more land.

The Ottawa were peaceful Indians who tried to live in harmony with settlers and lumbermen. In 1856 Charles McKie was one of the first settlers who received a government track of land in Bridgeton Township in section 18, near Maple Island. He later reflected on the kindness of the Indians to him and his family when he first arrived. He had made a deposit and was given 30 days to build a house on the land. On Easter Sunday he and his fellow lumbermen had a work bee to construct his house. The Indians located in the area urged Mr. McKie to allow his wife and two little children to stay with them until the home was completed. He accepted their offer and his family had shelter with the Indians until they could move into their home. Years later it was still important to Mr. Mckie that others knew about the help given to his family by the Indians.

Prior to Mr. McKie's arrival in 1856 much had transpired that turned the lives of the Native Americans upside down. Michigan was incorporated into a territory of the United States from 1805 until 1837, at which time it was granted statehood. After the War of 1812 there was a great demand for land in Michigan, mostly for speculative purposes, as a reward for military service. Two million acres of land in the territory were set aside at the end of the war for volunteers. Each man was entitled to 160 acres.

But the men sent to survey the land faced immense difficulties. They were afraid of the Indians, the winter weather was extremely bitter, and the marshes and swamps forbidding. Even so, when Michigan became a state, its population was still mostly made up of fur traders, Jesuit missionaries, and Native Americans. It wasn't until the opening of the Erie Canal that Michigan's population began to grow, for it was then possible to reach Michigan via Albany.

There were treaties, acts, and laws galore. Wading through all the details of these treaties could make readers want to throw up their hands in surrender. And the Native Americans could not even read the documents. Treaties ceding land to the government from various Indian tribes began with the Treaty of Greenville in 1795. Some others were Governor Hull's Treaty of 1805, the Treaty of Saginaw of 1819, two Treaties of Chicago in 1821 and 1833, Carey Mission in 1828, the Treaty of Washington in 1836, Treaty with the Potawatomi in 1837, the Treaty of La Pointe in 1842, and the 1855 Treaty of Detroit. Also there was an important Supreme Court case in 1823 which held that private citizens could not buy land directly from Native Americans. This forced the Native Americans to sell their land directly to the United States government. In 1842, by signing the Treaty of La Pointe, all rights to land within the state had been surrendered. These treaties, while complex, are worth reading because of the far-reaching impact they had on our nation, our state, and the Native American population.

In 1821 in terms with the United States government the Ottawa, Chippewa, and Potawatomi ceded all lands south of the Grand River allowing for only small reservations. Later, by signing the Treaty of Washington in 1836, the Michigan Ottawa and Chippewa tribes gave away much of their remaining land in the Upper and Lower Peninsulas, which included more than 13 million acres north of the Grand River.

Joesph 'Truckee' Troutier was chosen as one of the representatives in a delegation of Indians that traveled to Washington D.C. in 1836 to negotiate the treaty. Even though Truckee was half Ottawa, when he got to Washington he refused to say he was Indian and claimed to be only French, for reasons not known. By doing so he gave up his right to a stipend of $1000 in cash and an annual income for twenty years. However, as always, he seemed to prosper. After the treaty Truckee and two other fur traders, Baddeau and Lasley, made huge profits by sending goods to be sold to the Indians in Grand Rapids where they went to receive their semi-annual allotments and, thus, would have cash in hand.

The treaty was fraught with problems and the Native Americans quickly became dissatisfied. Fraud in the allotment process led to legal battles that lasted for 150 years. Some of the Native Americans who signed the treaty were later killed, presumably by other Native Americans who opposed the signing.

On January 26, 1837 the way had been cleared of Native American land ownership and Michigan became our 26th state. It met the requirements of having a population of 60,000 white residents. Blacks, and Indians were not counted. At the time of statehood the population was approximately 200,000. The land office in Ionia, Michigan was opened shortly after and the land boom began. With the ink barely dry on statehood, the problem of still having Indians on land being sold to settlers had to be resolved. Thus came one of the saddest parts in the history of our state. The Removal Act of 1830 was put into action.

Previously it was assumed by many that the Native Americans could become 'civilized' and assimilated with the white population. But newly elected President Andrew Jackson held that this was not possible. He began to aggressively push his agenda for removing all Native Americans living east of the Mississippi to Indian Territory on the west side of the river. Though contentiously fought against by many, the Indian Removal Act was passed May 30, 1830. In that year the Indian population statistics for the Michigan Territory was 29,060.

Almost all Native American tribes, no matter where they lived, have faced removal at some time. Most Americans are familiar with the 'Trail of

Tears' endured by the Cherokee in 1838 when they were forcibly removed from the Smoky Mountains to Oklahoma. Of the 15,000 Cherokee who made this trip about 4000 died. In the same year the Potawatomi had their own forced removal which they call 'The Trail of Death'.

The Potawatomi lived around the southern end of Lake Michigan encompassing parts of Michigan, Indiana, and Illinois. In the 1836 Treaty of Washington there was a clause agreeing to removal. That time came in 1838. The Potawatomi had sided with the British in the War of 1812 so there was already anger among the white settlers. When time came for them to leave, three chiefs refused to go. They were put in jail-like cages on wagons pulled by horses. One hundred armed men forced the rest to follow on horseback or walk. By the time they reached their destination in Kansas, forty-two had died. Most of these were children dying from typhoid.

The Ottawa and Ojibwa were also being squeezed out of their land and became more and more restricted as to where they could relocate. The 1836 treaty stated that the Native Americans had no right to stay on reservation land after 1841 without the express approval of the United States government. There was no guarantee these lands would not be sold to settlers. The Ottawa, unlike other tribes, were not given reservations of their own. They were strongly opposed to removal. Some attached themselves to other tribes and lived on reservations, while others moved to parts of Michigan that were still mostly uninhabited.

The Ottawa were more spread out than the Potawatomi, which made it more difficult for them to be gathered up. They tried to adapt by growing and selling crops to the new settlers. They used their annuities to buy land, thinking this would keep them safe from removal. They made friends with missionaries who were strongly against removal as well. These missionaries obtained land for the Ottawa by taking their cash annuities and buying the land in their names. Others pooled their money and bought land under one owner. Sometimes this was a person who was only part Indian. Then the property was shared by the whole group.

Chapter Two: The Treaty Years and Statehood

The last treaty of 1855 ended the Indian removal threat in Michigan and allowed for new reservations to be made. Oceana and Mason counties soon had their own reservations. It was not until 1924 that Native Americans received citizenship through the Indian Citizenship Act. Even then, they were not allowed to vote as voting rights were considered a state's right issue separate from citizenship. Finally, in 1953, Maine, as the last state in the Union to accept Native American citizenship, gave them the right to vote.

Chapter Four

The Boom

Perched at the mouth of the Muskegon River were squatters, Chicago speculators who waited in anticipation of the final bell of statehood to ring, and for the opening of the Ionia Land Office. Other squatters were similarly posted on various rivers north of the Grand River, including the Manistee. The leadership of the Muskegon speculators fell to Hiram Pierson and Henry Pennoyer. Their interest was timber.

Purchasing land for sixteen cents an acre allowed the lumbermen to move quickly across the landscape. Logging camps and sawmills abounded. Henry's brother Augustus Pennoyer opened the first sawmill for the Muskegon Lumber Company on Pennoyer Creek. Soon a second sawmill was built at Croton. By 1884 there were forty-seven sawmills on Muskegon Lake alone.

Besides the Pennoyers, other commonly occurring names at this time were Squier, Brooks, Newell, McBride, Knight, Hackley, Merrill, and Ryerson. We see these names on roads, buildings, parks, and schools to this day. A look at old plat maps reveals the vast amount of land that was owned by lumbermen. Once cleared, the land was sold to settlers for farming.

Many of today's roads were built on old logging trails, which were originally made to connect logging camps with one another. This seems to have been the case with Ryerson Road, which becomes 104th when it crosses into Bridgeton Township, one mile from Dickinson and Sitka territory. Martin Ryerson was a prominent road builder, having built the first road connecting Muskegon to Grand Rapids in 1847. He did so at his own expense, and followed the route of an old Indian trail from Muskegon Lake to Ravenna where it met up with an existing road to Grand Rapids.

Ryerson also had his name on a rural school located at the corner of Ryerson and Brickyard Roads. Neva Zerlaut, born in Sitka in 1897, was a teacher there. The school was still in operation when I was a child and the building, now converted to a private home, still exists

In 1834, at the age of sixteen, Martin Ryerson left his home in New Jersey and worked his way to Muskegon. After a short time, working the fur trading post of Louis Baddeau on Muskegon Lake, he moved on. In 1836 he became a clerk for none other than Joseph 'Truckee' Troutier for eight dollars a month. Later, when Ryerson had established his Ryerson, Hills, and Company lumber business he continued to buy his supplies from Truckee.

When Ryerson arrived at Maple Island the Ottawa Chief was Owoniscum, soon to be followed by Chief Kenewegisheks. Ryerson became enamored with the Native Americans, quickly learning their language and customs. In 1842 he married an Indian woman, whose name is unknown. A daughter, Mary, was born in 1843. Unfortunately the mother died in childbirth. In 1844 he married again to a half Indian woman named Louise M. Duverney, who, it is rumored, was the sister of Indian Bill. Louisa also died in childbirth in Kalamazoo in route to Chicago. Louisa and infant daughter were buried in Grand Haven.

Ryerson married a third time to Mary A. Campau. Their son Antoine was born in 1856 and lived to adulthood. By this time Ryerson had established his Ryerson Hills Farm on Maple Island. He built a mansion on the property along with thirteen barns. The farm provided food for his employees and the barns served as stables for the numerous horses and oxen needed to operate the lumbering business. He owned several thousand acres of land in Bridgeton Township and in nine other townships in Newaygo County. After his third wife's death he sold Ryerson Hills Farm to P. G. Cooley, finder of the previously mentioned skeleton and cross. At the time of his death in 1887 Ryerson was estimated to be worth four million dollars. This was a far cry from the man who began working for eight dollars a month.

The people who followed the lumbering trade were not all speculators. A large number of our ancestors were merely people looking for a fresh start and a chance, many for the first time, to own their own land. They were mostly interested in agriculture. Working the pines was just a means to an end. My great, great uncle Narzis Steiner was among them. He arrived in New York in 1853 from Bavaria. His sister Elizabeth Steiner Zerlaut, my great-great- grandmother, a widow, also came with seven children who were mostly young adults. Narzis worked various jobs until coming to Muskegon, where he worked in the saw mills. During the winter months he was in the employ of Ryerson, Hills, and Company as a cook in the camps. After two years he was able to preempt land in section 5 of Bridgeton Township, near the present day corner of Dickinson Road and 96th Street. He was one of the first to clear land in that area.

Charles McKie also wanted a chance to own his own land. He was born in Canada near Montreal. At the age of 23 he began working his way west at various jobs in farming and also worked as a millwright. McKie preempted his land in 1856. Michigan was federal land by then and the U. S. government had control over its dispersal. In 1839 the land of Newaygo County opened up for purchase for the first time. For days large numbers of men were camped out in front of the Ionia Land Office anticipating its opening. The hopeful buyers had to fill out an application for the particular tract of land they wanted. Tracts were sold for $1.25 an acre. Working for the lumber companies probably gave its employees a good chance to view available land. Sometimes all that was necessary to apply was payment itself, but most times it required the buyer to be a native-born citizen OR to declare his intention to become a U. S. citizen. An exception was made for military bound warrants where service was the only requirement. After the application was filed, a survey of the tract of land was completed, payment made, and a final certificate, known as a land patent, was given. In the case of Mr. McKie a condition was attached that erecting a house on the land within a certain time period must take place.

Chapter Four: The Boom

Many of the men worked the logging camps from late fall until spring. In summer they worked their properties and returned to the camps again in the fall. They continued this pattern of seasonal work until their farms were able to sustain them.

The lumbermen built their camps, and then proceeded to make roads to the stands of trees they planned to harvest. These roads were watered down when the weather turned cold and it started to snow. Icy roads made it possible to use huge sleds to transport logs. There were many jobs in the camps: cooks, blacksmiths, teamsters, rafters, sawyers. The work in the camps was difficult and hazardous. Cutting and moving logs was an enormous and dangerous job; some of the logs measured eight feet in diameter! Breaking up log jams in the spring killed or injured many.

The camp conditions were not very desirable. The men slept on ticks made of straw. Wires were strung about to hang wet clothing. There was little in the way of sanitary conditions. The discomfort in the end, though, was worth it. Owning land free and clear was the reward.

Not all logging camps were big operations. Many in the Sitka area had their own camps. Once land owners purchased their property they had to continue to clear it to make it suitable for farming. Selling off timber was a good way to provide a supplemental income.

My great grandfather, Joseph A. Zerlaut, a nephew of Narzis Steiner, ran a logging operation as well. He owned the land originally preempted by Narzis. He also owned unbroken forest land in Sheridan Township, which had to be timbered. It wasn't enough to just saw down the trees. Once the logs were gone, stumps then had to be pulled using a stump puller. The puller was a large derrick-like contraption that got its power from a horse walking around it in a circle; an arduous task to say the least.

Robert Jibson also followed the lumber trade to Sitka. Coming from England, he and his wife, Ann Buttle, came to America in 1849. He worked as a shingle-maker. Upon preempting land in Bridgeton

Township in 1861, he continued to buy land, finally owning 440 acres by 1880. He set up camp behind the area where the Jibson School was later located. It was called the Jibson Rollaway. The steep gully hills along Brooks Creek allowed logs to be rolled into the water and moved to the Muskegon River and on to the lumber mills on Muskegon Lake. He had his log mark registered in Muskegon County in 1865. 'RJ' was stamped in the center of each end of the logs. This proved ownership once the logs reached the mills. Traces of the logs being rolled down to Brooks Creek still remained when I was young.

Though the lumbering slowed down greatly during the Civil War, it regained its strength at war's end. Lumbering continued into the very late 1800s. A fire in Sitka destroyed 150,000 shingles belonging to the Mills Bros. of Holton in 1890. John Ady Jr. was severely injured at his father's mill at Sitka in 1891. Ransom Squier, originally from New York, had a mill in section 6 of Bridgeton after preempting ten acres in 1860. In 1892 Robert Kempf set up his own mill. Everyone, it seems, got in on the lumbering action.

The increasing number of people moving west created a growing demand for more and more lumber to build homes and businesses. Wood was also needed to stoke the steamships. Then came the devastating Chicago fire of 1871. The strong winds at the time made it easy for the fire to travel quickly through the city. The fire destroyed an area about four miles in length. Three hundred people were killed and more than 100,000 left homeless. Two thirds of the buildings at the time were made of wood and had wooden shingles for roofs. Once it was over, all those buildings had to be replaced. The timber forests were hit hard for their wood. The need, it seems, was insatiable.

What did the people of the time feel about all this lumbering? There were mixed opinions. The Fremont Times often mentioned the lumber camps. In July 1878, for instance, Ryerson Hills camp at Worcester was said to be employing eighty men and shipping logs at the rate of 100,000 feet per day. They were paying their pine wooders $18 to $25 a month.

Chapter Four: The Boom

On April 30, 1878 the newspaper reported: 'Ryerson, Hills, and Co. have made another 'grab' and picked up 6000 acres of pine land, adjoining the 4000 acres they own north of Newaygo. They paid E. Wood of New York $100,000 for it. R. H. & Co. is one of the best firms that have ever done any lumbering business in this county.' But by October 1879 the view of the Fremont Times of Ryerson, Hills & Co. seems to have changed. 'Ryerson & Hills have a strong 'army' in camp a few miles east of Fremont. That army is dealing out 'death and destruction' to millions of pine timber.'

In 1877 the railroads began moving lumber. It was easier to haul logs from the interior via the rails. Also, by using the railroads the loggers no longer had to wait for winter weather, they could haul logs throughout the year. The forests were finally depleted and by the early 1900s the lumbering business drew to a close. Small operations continued for a time, but the last major run on the Muskegon River was in 1905 and the last sawmill on Muskegon Lake was closed in 1910.

During this period those not lumbering, or only partly so, were working in earnest to establish their farms. By 1860 it was going well for many of the inhabitants of the Sitka area. But then something happened that many of the newly-arrived immigrants surely had never dreamed of when they came to America, leaving behind their homelands for a better future. The United States entered into a civil war and great numbers of men from the area were called into service.

Chapter Five

The Civil War

Imagine struggling to come to a new country and having just achieved your dream of owning your own land and building a home. You still have land to clear for farming, but you are up to the challenge. Maybe a wife and children also work beside you. Life is hard, but it is good. Imagine the life of your family, now left behind, trying to fend for itself as you leave for a war that was never part of your plans. That was the situation for many of those who came to Sitka.

When war broke out in 1861, there were 468 men eligible for duty in Newaygo County; of them, 81 were from Bridgeton Township. (Sheridan Township was not created until 1867, after the war.) Bridgeton Township easily met its quota. A year after the war began, 79 men had voluntarily enrolled for service. The average age was twenty-seven.

By the latter part of the war four drafts were needed to fill Newaygo County's quota, the last being in March, 1865. These men, however, were not needed due to the ending of the war. Such was the experience of Heinrich (Henry) Zerlaut, son of Elizabeth Steiner Zerlaut. At age 22, Henry was drafted into Company A of the 16th Michigan Infantry. He was mustered out three months later without seeing action. Many others were not so lucky.

In 1852 Christoph (Christopher) Kempf came to America from Germany. Christopher, like so many others who came, changed his occupation, from weaver, to working in the lumber mills in Muskegon. He remained there for nine years and met and married Katherine Kopf in 1858. By 1860 he had purchased 80 acres of forest land near Sitka, eventually owning 620 acres. But this land would first have to be cleared for farming.

Chapter Five: The Civil War

In preparation for clearing the land, trees were girdled by encircling the trunks with cuts through the bark so they would not leaf out. Once the trees were lumbered they began planting crops around the stumps. It might be several years before they attempted to remove the stumps, allowing the roots to die so they would more easily break off as the stump was pulled.

To pull the stump they employed a derrick like structure operated by horsepower. The stump puller was very heavy and required three husky men to set the three poles, which were tee-pee like in nature. Inside from the top a very large screw was dropped down to the center of the stump. From the top of the "teepee" another pole was attached that could rotate when pulled by a team of horses. The operation was much like using a corkscrew to open a bottle of wine. It might take all day to pull a large stump. When the stump was out they reversed the direction of the horses to get the screw back out.

Christopher's lumbering and farming work enabled him to send money back to family in Germany. Eventually his parents, Johann and Margarita, came to America. Christopher's two brothers, Johann Nicolaus (known also as Nick), Fred, and his sister Margarita (Margaret) also emigrated.

Nick came to this country in 1855. He filed papers of intent to become a U. S. citizen in 1860 and by 1861 had preempted 40 acres of land adjoining Christopher's. His recently widowed mother lived with him and served as his housekeeper. He continued to work in the mills and work his land. The rapid speed with which the Kempf family was able to come to this country and become land owners speaks well of their hard work and persistence. All seemed to be going well for this industrious twenty-two year old, but one month after purchasing his land he was volunteering for service. He enlisted with more than thirty other men from Newaygo County in the newly organized Company C, 3rd Michigan Infantry Regiment.

Nick's brother, Fred, was only fifteen when Nick volunteered, and was considered too young for service. Christopher, however, being older than Nick, was of military age.

Christopher opted to avoid service in the same manner as future president, Grover Cleveland, and John D. Rockefeller. These men were healthy, and made eligible by being between the ages of 20 and 45, but were able to pay a substitute to serve in their place. The Enrollment Act of 1863 allowed draftees to pay a sum of three hundred dollars for a substitute for service. This was a hefty amount of money in the 1860s. The price demanded eventually soared to over a thousand dollars by war's end. When Christopher's time came to be drafted, he paid a substitute the three hundred dollars to be relieved of the obligation. That substitute, whose name is unknown, later died in action.

But one should not be too hasty to judge this decision. Many things must have weighed heavily on Christopher's mind. For one thing, by the time he was drafted, he had a widowed mother, a wife, and two young children—three year old Robert, and one year old Gustav—to think about. Fred was still at home, but he was only eighteen. Could he be entrusted with the care of the entire family, for who knew how long—weeks, months, years? After all, Nick had already been gone two years by then.

So many things would need to be done to make sure the family could survive the first winter: laying up of wood for heat and cooking, chinking the logs of the cabin to keep out the cold, hunting to replace stores of food. Remember, Sitka was not yet established. There was no store to buy supplies, no creamery, blacksmith shop, or post office—no church to give aid and comfort. There were few neighbors, and even fewer roads—simply trails through the woods—to get to someone for help. They would be on their own in the wilds of Michigan.

It is not known whether the women knew how to use a gun to hunt or for protection. Would that have been left up to the men until this point? Unknown men often wandered the forests. Many wild animals, such as bear and wolves, were about in the woods, as well. At the time of the Civil War, wolves were a big problem. My great aunt, Katie (Kempf) Zerlaut, wife of Herman Zerlaut, lived on the farm originally belonging to Elizabeth Steiner Zerlaut. She told of the claw marks left on the logs of the cabin one winter by wolves trying to get inside. A bounty on wolves existed during the Civil War. Two to five dollars per pelt was paid. This almost drove them to extinction—but that is a story for some other time. The point is that this could be a dangerous place!

Then there was Nick. It is not known if the family was aware of his circumstances, but things were not going well for him. Could the family afford to lose both Nick and Christopher? So Christopher stayed on and took care of the home front. As for Nick, he had covered a lot of territory since his enlistment.

* * *

Early June 13, 1861: Ten companies of the 3rd Michigan Infantry Regiment left their quarters in Grand Rapids and followed their officers and its regimental band to the train station. Two special trains took them to Detroit. During the night the regiment boarded two boats and made for Cleveland, Ohio. Again by rail, they continued on through Pennsylvania and Maryland, finally arriving at their destination on June 16. They were in Washington, D.C.

Three days of travel must have left them tired, hungry, and edgy. Sick of drills and traveling, they were ready to get on with their task of settling this conflict. They set up their first camp, called Camp McConnell, after the regiment's colonel, on the bluffs overlooking the Potomac. Later the name changed to Camp Blair after the governor of the state of Michigan. Patriotic fervor was high in this early part of the war. Three days later they were on their way to Manassas, Va.

It wasn't long before all the hoopla, the bands, the crowds and the cheering gave way to the realities of war. Anyone with knowledge of Civil War battles will shudder when reading the list of conflicts in which these men participated: both Battles of Bull Run, Siege of Yorktown, Battle of Fair Oaks (also known as Seven Pines), Malvern Hill, Battle of Fredericksburg, Battle of Chancellorsville, Battle of Gettysburg, Mine Run Campaign, Battle of the Wilderness, Battle of Spotsylvania Court House, Harris Farm—Fredericksburg Road, and the Battle of Cold Harbor, as well as many other minor conflicts.

Nick's troubles began at the battle of Malvern Hill, Virginia, about fifteen miles southeast of Richmond, on July 1, 1862. Many of the 3rd Regiment were scattered during the battle and Nick was listed as missing in action. Eventually he was reunited with his regiment at Camp Alexandria, Virginia. He was put on detached duty working as a teamster for the Brigade wagon train for several months.

During the night on May 1, 1863, through dense forests, the 3rd Regiment attacked at Chancellorsville, only to be scattered again. Thousands died on both sides. Due to the darkness, many men were killed by friendly fire.

On July 2, 1863 they clashed with the enemy in the bloody Gettysburg massacre at 'Peach Orchard', and were driven to the height of 'Cemetery Ridge', the 3rd regiment suffered their greatest losses to date at Gettysburg.

Spring 1864 took the regiment north once more, fighting the Battle of the Wilderness, where four Newaygo men were casualties. On May 12, 1864 the infantry struck at daybreak in a musket massacre at Spotsylvania, Virginia. Two more Newaygo men were disabled; one was Nick Kempf. He was felled by a bullet, seriously wounding him in his forearm. This was just one day before his three year term of service was completed. Upon his discharge, it was also noted that he had acute inflammation of the kidneys.

Notwithstanding his wounds, Pvt. Nick Kempf tried to reenlist, but was denied. He was mustered out June 27, 1864 and returned home to his mother who cared for him. Though she did all she could, it was too late; gangrene had set in. Besides his family, two former members of Company H, Joseph Schuler and Gustave Arndt, attended him at his death. He died July 6, 1864, having served admirably. He had never been able to complete his citizenship, nor his dream of farming his own land. A pension of eight dollars a month was given to his mother.

* * *

Bavaria, Germany 1848: Elizabeth Steiner Zerlaut became a widow with seven young children to support; the oldest, Veronica, was only 13. An older stepdaughter, Anna, was also living with them. Elizabeth's husband Joseph had operated a nail forge business which Elizabeth continued running after his death, but three years later, as an unwed mother, she gave birth to a boy, whom she named Gabriel (Otto) Steiner. The inhabitants of her small mountain village of Sonthofen condemned and shunned her for her transgression. She was shut out of association with other colleagues and forced into bankruptcy.

To her credit, she did not throw in the towel. Instead, in 1852 she contacted her brother, Narzis Steiner, who was working as a baker in New York. At that time she was faced with many debts. The Bavarian State Archives show a collection of unpaid bills, settlement of which the community of Sonthofen demanded, including, among others, bills from the baker for bread debts and bills from the butcher for meat debts that needed to be settled before she could migrate. Eventually she and her brother organized her voyage across the ocean to America with her entire flock of children. What an undertaking that must have been!

They settled initially in Rhode Island where Elizabeth's oldest son, Joseph, only fourteen years old, took work in the woolen mills. The migration to Muskegon, where Joseph and his Uncle Narzis had found work in the saw mills, occurred in 1858.

Narzis was able to preempt 240 acres of land spread across Sheridan and Bridgeton Townships in 1860-61. He soon moved his sister and her family to land he had cleared. In 1863 he sold 118 acres of his land to his sister Elizabeth for $1.60 per acre. By that time Joseph was gone, having volunteered for service in 1862 at the age of twenty-two.

Joseph joined the Sixth Michigan Cavalry, Co. H. This regiment was attached to the Army of the Potomac, part of the Michigan Brigade, commanded by General George Custer. The men were detained for two months until the quota of twelve hundred twenty-nine officers and men was filled. Forty of these men would be from Newaygo County.

Finally, the quota filled, the long tedious delay ended and they were on the move. The regiment left Grand Rapids, traveling by horseback, to meet up with Sheridan's command in Washington, D.C. The regiment was fully mounted and equipped, but they were not armed. Their job, when they arrived, was to protect the capitol and President Lincoln, from the threatening rebel army.

They were finally armed with Spenser Repeating Rifles, which were far superior to the weapons of the Confederate Cavalry. The Michigan troops were the first to engage at Gettysburg. Joseph was unable to participate at Gettysburg, being severely ill at the time.

Throughout 1863 the Sixth was constantly on the move, and engaged in action. Joseph told of having a cannon ball explode behind him, killing at least 14 men and knocking his hat off, but otherwise he survived the blast unharmed. Another time he had his horse shot out from under him, then had to run over half a mile to escape the pursuing Rebels behind him. His run of luck ran out October 19 at Buckland Mills, Va.

General Lee's army was withdrawing from near Manassas and the Union cavalry gave pursuit. The Rebel cavalry set up an ambush near Chestnut Hill and the Union cavalry was routed. Federal troops scattered and were chased for five miles. This 'retreat' became known as the

'Buckland Races'.

Joseph received crippling rifle fire in this battle. The bullet entered his left leg above the knee, traveled upward, and exited through his hip. He was taken to a hospital in Washington, D.C., thirty-five miles away, where he remained for six weeks. While recovering, President Lincoln came and made the rounds of the wounded. He shook hands with the men, including Joseph, and thanked them for their heroism.

Joseph was then sent back to Muskegon where he was hospitalized for two more months. Notwithstanding his injuries, he was promoted to Full Corporal and sent back to active duty.

In 1864 the Sixth gained another member of the family. Narzis Steiner, then age 38, enlisted in Co. I, 6th Michigan Cavalry. He and his nephew fought in many of the same battles. They saw action in the Battle of the Wilderness, Battle of Yellow Tavern and Battle of Winchester. At Trevillian Station Narzis fell from his horse and was injured. He was then taken prisoner and remained in captivity several days until he was finally able to escape. Joseph and Narzis went on to fight in the Battle of Cedar Creek, Appomattox, and many other battles.

After the surrender of General Lee the Sixth returned to Washington, D.C. They marched down Pennsylvania Ave. in the Grand Review on May 23, 1865. The regimental flag for the Sixth Michigan Cavalry displayed the motto: 'Fear Not Death—Fear Dishonor.'

By the end of the war the Sixth had lost 7 officers and 128 enlisted men in battle, and 251 more to disease.

* * *

Oh, to be home again! Unfortunately for some, it was not yet time to retire the regimental flag.

The summer of 1865 found many Newaygo County veterans mustering out, having fulfilled their three year enlistment. However, the Sixth, including Joseph, was sent west, via railroad and riverboat, to Ft. Leavenworth, Kansas. From there they were ordered farther west, across the plains, to Ft. Laramie. There they fought the Indians in an effort to suppress the war being waged by several Indian tribes. The regiments involved were later grouped together and called the 1st Michigan Veteran Cavalry.

The Veteran Cavalry constructed 'Fort Connor' as a supply depot during the Powder River Expedition. A detachment of the regiment guarded James A. Sawyer's wagon train in the Sawyer Fight of August and September 1865.

Later, Joseph reflected on the fighting in which he was involved. He said fellow cavalry men were shot from their horses, where they were trampled underfoot, while he and others were forced to abandon them.

On September 24th, most of the regiment, including Joseph A. Zerlaut, were mustered out at Ft. Leavenworth and finally allowed to return home. He walked with a painful limp the rest of his life. Those whose enlistments did not expire until February 1866, including Narzis Steiner, were transferred to the First Michigan Cavalry until March.

* * *

Before leaving the story of the Michigan Cavalry, there is one more citizen of the Sitka area that needs to be mentioned. Antoine Troutier, son of Joseph 'Truckee' Troutier, enlisted in the 10th Michigan Cavalry, September 1, 1863. He was 25 years old. He was well known for his life in the woods and on the water. He had already spent many years logging and rafting. He also operated a flatbed steamer. Ten days after enlisting he was mustered out at Grand Rapids, Michigan. The charge: desertion.

No record has been found of any punishment. He did return to the

Sitka area again, working the mills. Like his father he married several times and had seven children. He died at age 60 in 1899 and was referred to as 'the last of the real river men.'

* * *

On the east side of Sitka two more families sent loved ones to war. Guernsey Hull and his wife, Lydia, arrived in 1861 from Medina, Ohio. They brought their three children, Laban, 22, Edmund, 20, and Adelia, 15. Shortly after arriving, Edmund enlisted in Co. C, 26th Michigan Infantry. He saw intense fighting in Virginia. Edmund survived the war, mustering out in July 1865. Though his family remained in the area for several years, no further mention of Edmund can be found.

George Cotham settled in the Sitka area in 1864 as a newlywed. He and his wife, Elizabeth, were married in England in 1851 and emigrated to America the same year. By then they had two children, Sarah and George Jr. The war was nearly over when he enlisted in Co. E, 15th Michigan Infantry in March of 1864 at the age of thirty-eight. After Lee surrendered at Appomattox in June 1865, he deserted with nine other Newaygo men. The war being finished, they had had enough and saw no reason to fill out the three year term of their enlistment.

At long last the war was over, changing the lives of many forever. The people of the Sitka area were nothing if not resilient. The men returned with their wounds, worn out bodies, and haunting memories to their interrupted lives, and once again began building a community in which to raise their families.

Chapter Six

Moving Forward

After the Civil War the population of the Sitka area grew quickly. Unmarried soldiers returned and found spouses, and numerous others decided to move to the area and settle down.

One month before enlisting, Heinrich (Henry) Zerlaut married Adelia Hull, his neighbor and the sister of Edmund. Henry was trained as a barber. Upon his return from the war he and Adelia moved to Muskegon where he opened a barbershop. They would return to Sitka nine years later, enduring many hardships.

Brother Joseph A. Zerlaut married Anna Bing of Muskegon on February 17, 1866. She had emigrated from Germany with her family when she was seventeen years old. At the time of her marriage she was working as a domestic. They lived with Joseph's mother, Elizabeth, his three sisters, and younger brother Gabriel, who had all come together from Germany, and worked the farm as a family.

Though not from the area originally, three brothers, Lewis, Holly, and Samuel Crawford, found it a good place to make a new start. They contributed greatly to the community for many years. All were Civil War veterans.

Lewis had been part of Co. B, 27th Michigan Volunteers Infantry. He was discharged with a disability after the Battle of Vicksburg. He arrived with his wife of one year, Elizabeth Leonardson, and stayed for ten years. He involved himself with road building, which was sorely needed, especially with all the new arrivals.

The early roads were taken care of by the pathmaster system. Each spring a pathmaster would be elected, who would then be in charge of collecting the poll tax for roads. This was levied at one dollar or more for each male over eleven years of age, based upon the individual's holdings. If the person was unable to pay they could work off the tax by helping to fix the roads. Filling in of holes, clearing brush, and adding culverts were some of the projects that were done. Even then, the roads could prove to be extremely dangerous.

This can be seen in the story of Henry Wilde, who in 1856, at the age of 27, boarded a ship called the Hammonia in Hamburg, Germany and departed for New York. His occupation on the ship's roster was given as Landman, or someone who works the land. After arriving he made his way to Milwaukee, Wisconsin where he married Martha Bertha Wachlin, a native of Prussia. Within a few years they were living in Sitka with three young children, having 40 acres each in Bridgeton and Sheridan townships.

One late November day in 1878 Henry drove his horse and wagon to the town we now know as Fremont. It was probably a day-long round trip, with winter weather approaching, and early darkness. He was detained much later than he had planned and started for home when it was quite late. Only one mile outside of town he was thrown from his wagon; one of the wheels passed over his head.

Both Drs. Ellis and Nafe were sent for and found him greatly injured. He was taken back to town and thought to be able to recover from his accident. However, later that night he took a turn for the worst and passed away.

The newspaper article describing the accident warned readers of rough roads and stumps that could bring danger to those traveling. In fact, in the next few years many reminders were printed about the importance of being cautious on the roads.

The Wilde's had already suffered many losses. By the time Henry died they had already lost at least three young children. His wife was pregnant with another child at the time of his death. Henry and several children are still buried in the family cemetery surrounded by a clump of trees just south of the old homestead in an open field, across from the Sitka Methodist Church.

* * *

Holly Crawford came to Sitka and stayed until his death in 1913. This had not been his original plan. Both Lewis and Holly left home to work at a very young age after their father died unexpectedly, leaving their mother with eight children to support. By the time Holly was a young man he had decided to head for California. He taught school and worked on farms in between school sessions, making his way as far as Kansas; but when the Civil War broke out, he felt compelled to return to Illinois, where he had been working for an uncle, and enlist. He joined the 39th Illinois Infantry Regiment. When fighting began many in the regiment mutinied; three months later the regiment was dissolved.

Not one to give up easily, he joined the 11th Illinois Volunteer Infantry. He was wounded at Ft. Donelson and hospitalized. Along with his brother, his regiment fought in Vicksburg in a siege that lasted forty-six days, where he was in charge of the brigade colors.

At the surrender of Vicksburg he was selected to march into the captured city, but was much too ill and was again hospitalized. Holly was honorably discharged with the rank of sergeant.

Upon settling in the area he became county clerk, township supervisor, and spent twenty years as Justice of the Peace. He was also the postmaster of Sitka for sixteen years. He and his wife, Luella (Nelson), together raised nine children, many of whom made their own contributions to the community. Their son, Guy Crawford, was the last pathmaster of Sheridan Township.

Samuel F. Crawford enlisted in Co. A., Michigan 1st Infantry. A year later he was wounded in Harrison's Landing, Va. and was mustered out.

With the same tenacity as his brother Holly, he refused to quit. He reenlisted in 1864 and served another year and a half, leaving service as a full Corporal.

Under the Homestead Act Samuel purchased 160 acres in Sheridan Township in 1873. However, by 1880 he was living with Holly and family. Samuel applied for a Civil War pension in 1887 and on the form was listed as an invalid. Perhaps his war injuries had made it too difficult for him to continue farming. He left Sitka to live with Lewis in Ashland Township, where he later died of heart disease in 1900. Samuel never married.

As for Lewis, in 1875 he and Elizabeth Crawford moved to Ashland Township where they farmed and he became a Christian Advent minister. Their son, Fayette, however, remained in Sitka until the end of the century, adding his own touch to the growth of the area.

These three brothers, their families, mother Lydia, and sisters Ann and Martha, were part of a growing number of families coming to the area. As the population increased, the people felt it was time to have an official name for their community. Seward's Folly provided the inspiration.

Chapter Seven

Sitka and the Alaska Purchase

The United States acquired Alaska from the Russians in 1867. Russia was in deep financial trouble and anxious to sell the territory, thinking if they got into a war with the United Kingdom, this territory might be seized and taken from them at great financial loss.

Public opinion on the whole was positive. Many thought the purchase would prove to be a great economic boon to the United States. There were naysayers, of course, who nicknamed the deal 'Seward's Folly', after then Secretary of State William H. Seward.

The treaty easily passed by the U. S. Senate with 37 votes for, and 2 opposed. The cost was 7.2 million dollars and added 586,412 square miles of territory to the United States.

The transfer ceremony took place October 18, 1867 in Sitka, the Russian capital of Alaska. It remained the capital of the United States territory until the head of government was moved to Juneau in 1906.

The Alaska Purchase was big news in 1867 and by the time it all filtered down to the people living in the wilderness, it caused great excitement. Thus, in 1868, the little community in Newago County, Michigan officially adopted the name of Sitka in honor of the Alaska Purchase. A Sitka post office was opened December 14, 1868 in the home of Holly Crawford. As yet there were no stores or community buildings. All business and every service, from marriages to funerals, took place in the homes of the settlers. But the community now had a name.

Chapter Eight

Educating the Young

The residents of Sitka, on the whole, were hard working, civic-minded, and educated people. Making voyages across the ocean in the 1800s to start new lives could not have been done easily; many sacrifices were made to undergo such an ordeal. As the child population began to increase, they began thinking about what they wanted for their children in this new land.

In the early 1870s Newaygo County began setting up school districts. The beginning boundaries of the districts were adjusted numerous times to accommodate changes in the population; both in size and in the areas where the people tended to gather and settle. Sitka encompassed two school districts.

In 1871 District #4—later called the Kempf School—was originally a large district encompassing areas from both Sheridan and Bridgeton Townships. By 1876 District #4 had been split or added to several times, but the Kempf School remained in Sheridan Township.

Also known as the Matthews School in the earlier days, it was originally located in a field across from Christopher Kempf's farm, in section 32 northeast of Sitka. Nothing is known of the structure used for the school, but later another site was purchased from Fred and Laura Matthews and a new brick building was constructed on the southern end of their property.

Fred Matthews was born in French speaking Quebec, Canada in 1835. At the age of seventeen, with only fifteen dollars in his pocket, he left with a friend to set out for Chicago. His friend's courage failed him after a time and he returned home, but Fred persevered. By the time he reached Chicago he was penniless. To make matters worse he knew no one and was unable to speak the language. He was fortunate to meet a countryman who made him a guest in his home for three days until Fred could find employment.

After a year he pursued work in the lumbering business in Wisconsin. He remained there for two years, becoming a skilled wood worker. He left to visit a brother (Frank) in Muskegon in 1861. He decided to stay and preempted 160 acres of land in Sheridan Township.

Laura Lucinda Lee, not yet eighteen years old, became Fred's bride in 1872. She later wrote of moving to 'a wilderness, dotted here and there by tiny log cabins. The wild deer grazed in their meadows and foraged in their cornfields, and the mink, foxes, and weasels feasted on their domestic fowls.'

Besides making land available for the Kempf School, this couple was an intricate part of establishing religious services in the Sitka area, but their faith would be sorely tested, as we will soon see.

Robert Jibson sold one acre of land for $25 on the southwest corner of his farm for the development of Jibson School, District #3. The original building burned down, but a new one was erected in 1883.

Previous to the building of these schools, the education of children was conducted in individual homes. Future Jibson students met at August Socks (Sox) home across from the farm of Frederick (Ed) Ruprecht, approximately three quarters of a mile south of Sitka corners. For many years Sunday school was also convened at the Socks home. Guy Crawford remembered attending Sunday services after they were moved to the newly built Jibson School.

These buildings offered little in the way of comfort—having no electricity, running water, and only outhouses for sanitary purposes. They were more for shelter and a place to gather that wasn't as crowded or temporary as someone's home. In the case of the Kempf School, a neighbor, Will Young, daily provided water by carrying it to the school from his nearby farm. Ed Ruprecht, and later a member of the Freudenstein family, did the same for Jibson School. Eventually a deep well was dug at Jibson School and a small 'house' was built over it.

Wood also had to be provided by the community. It had to be chopped and stacked, ready for building a fire in the old potbellied stove early in the morning before the students arrived.

Teachers came and went, often staying only one term. Many of the teachers have names already familiar to us in the early years. The Kempf School employed David and John Crawford, Carrie Ruprecht, and Christina Kempf. The Jibson School also had Carrie Ruprecht, along with Neva Zerlaut, Mary Ruprecht, and Marion Jibson.

Pupil attendance was often sporadic. There was often bad weather and impassable roads. Sometimes the students would be needed at home to help with planting or harvesting crops. But no matter, the education of the young had started. There were now buildings where the community could meet or hold religious services. The town was starting to develop according to the needs of the people.

Chapter Nine

The Invisible Enemy

From the Fremont Indicator:

> *'Diphtheria is now raging at Grand Rapids, to rather an alarming extent.'* (February 12, 1879)
> *'Big influenza outbreak, stopping some schools.'* (February 26, 1879)
> *'Scarlet fever has broken out in southwestern part of Sheridan, and the school in that neighborhood* (Kempf) *has been closed by the order of the board of health. All necessary precautions will be taken to prevent the epidemic from spreading.'* (May 7, 1879)
> *'Hope scarlet fever does not reach Fremont. The doctors hate it more than smallpox.'* (May 7, 1879)
> *'Died of scarlet fever, May 1st, in Sheridan, Freddie, son of Mr. and Mrs. Frederick Matthews; aged six years and five months.'* (May 21, 1879)
> *'Diphtheria has taken away a good number of children this year.'* (November 5, 1879)
> *'Diphtheria rages down by 'the gully.'* (December 10, 1879)

During the latter quarter of the 1800s, epidemics of many kinds flourished in Sitka and in the state as a whole. Often there were multiple diseases threatening the settlers and their families at the same time. Once an epidemic appeared to have passed, a new one would come down upon them, or an old one would make a repeat appearance. Lack of medicines, vaccines, and knowledge about how diseases were spread allowed these epidemics to continue long into the 1900s.

Just the mention of diphtheria sent chills down the spine. Diphtheria is a bacterial infection that is easily spread via air, direct contact with an infected person, or touching contaminated objects. Some people can carry and spread the disease without any symptoms whatsoever.

Symptoms usually start within five days of exposure, beginning with a sore throat and fever. Next, white patches in the throat appear which

Chapter Nine: The Invisible Enemy

cause the lymph nodes to enlarge, the neck to swell, and air passages to close. Inflammation can occur in many other parts of the body as well. There were no treatments available. Some people were able to pull through; many did not.

Scarlet fever is another bacterial disease, which before antibiotics, was a major cause of death around the world. It is spread by inhaling the bacteria in the air. Symptoms include sore throat, high fever, and red rash. Later complications from the disease caused long term health problems, such as rheumatic fever and heart problems, which were often fatal at the time.

As the name implies, typhoid fever produces very high fevers. The profuse sweating from the fevers, along with severe diarrhea, can cause dehydration. Gastroenteritis as well as delirium is commonly associated with typhoid fever. The symptoms, if left untreated, last about four weeks.

Typhoid is all about sanitation. Lack of knowledge, hygiene, and deficient sanitary facilities compounded the spread of this disease. Water and food polluted by flying insects feasting on contaminated feces, and person to person contact, provided the path for the disease to take hold.

If you were lucky enough to avoid these diseases, whooping cough may have been your downfall. This highly contagious bacterial disease was often called the 100-day cough. Similar to a cold in the beginning, it led to severe fits of coughing, leaving the person gasping for breath. It is an airborne disease that can last several weeks.

Not to be left out, tuberculosis and flu were added to the mix. Just shaking the hand of a neighbor could prove deadly.

The cemeteries, both public and private, mark the sweep of these epidemics; and this does not take into account the number of unmarked graves still on ancestral farms, lost now to history.

These were the heartbreak years.

* * *

After the Civil War, Narzis Steiner removed himself from the Sitka area to Muskegon where he became a prominent business owner, running the Steiner House on Ottawa St. until his death in 1903. With his permission, his sister, Elizabeth Steiner Zerlaut, decided to sell her land to her oldest sons, Joseph A. and Heinrich.

The mortgage between Joseph and his mother is very specific in making sure her needs would be covered for the rest of her life. Joseph was to provide his mother each year with 150 pounds of pork, two barrels of flour, forty-eight pounds of butter, one quart of milk daily, and pay a sum of $12 annually for life. He also had to clear and fence three acres of land, work said land for three years, with all profits going to his mother, and erect a log cabin on the property within a year. In addition, she must receive one yoke of steer and one cow. What a negotiator she must have been!

It is to be remembered that she still had three adult daughters and a young son living with her at the time, so she was looking out for them as well.

Though no copy of Henry's contract has survived, it is known that he also bought 80 acres of land from his mother in 1867 for a sum of $500. Henry continued to live with his wife Adelia and children in Muskegon where his barbershop was located.

Ten short years later, much of this family would be gone.

As with the Chicago fire, the wooden buildings, piles of lumber and sawdust, fed the 1874 fire of Muskegon. A quarter of the business district and 200 homes were destroyed. Among them were the home and barbershop of Henry and Adelia. They returned to Sitka to the property he had purchased and Henry took up farming.

They brought with them three young children: Edmund, Grace, and

Chapter Nine: The Invisible Enemy

Jessie. Soon afterwards a son, Roy, was born. It is not known which of the diseases passed through these little bodies, but in 1877, while pregnant with another child to be called Ermina, Roy died. Ermina followed two years later. They were buried on the farm on the corner of Dickinson and 100th St. In 1890 Edmund also died.

The losses this family suffered took its toll. Soon after moving back to Sitka, Henry took out a series of mortgages against his property. He also began drinking heavily, as one after another of his children died. In March 1894 Adelia died; dropsy was listed as the cause—a 'cover all' cause of death often used at the time. There are family rumors that Adelia's death was a suicide. She was buried with the little children near the southeast corner of the house until they were eventually moved to the Holton Cemetery.

Only four months later, Henry died. Cause of death was also given as dropsy, but was most likely alcohol related. The day before Henry died he deeded his property to his brother for $1600. Joseph also paid off any mortgages that remained.

There were five remaining children upon their parents' death. Frederick died in 1900; Grace and Earl moved to the state of Washington, as far away from death and sadness as they could get, and Fay married and took refuge in Kalamazoo. Jessie also married, but later took her own life.

By 1900 there were no traces of Heinrich and his family left in Sitka. His property was eventually sold by Joseph to his son, Henry E. Zerlaut in 1901. This was later the home of my father, Harold, for 92 years, and still remains in the family.

Joseph and Anna Zerlaut were not without their own torments. By 1876 they had lost two children; gone were baby Frank and six month old Elizabeth. By 1877 most of the original Zerlaut family had been wiped out. Elizabeth Steiner Zerlaut, the tiny, feisty, widow, who braved the ocean with seven children in tow, was taken. Gone also were daughters Veronica, Theresa, and Josepha. They were all buried on the farm until the Holton cemetery was opened in 1880; Elizabeth and the two babies were moved and placed in one grave. The whereabouts of the three daughters' remains are unknown, as search for records and grave markers at the cemetery come up empty.

Of those making the journey across the ocean to start new lives in the wilderness, only Joseph, his sister Barbara, married and living in another part of the state, and younger brother Gabriel (Otto), were left. Otto disappeared form Sitka in the early 1900s and was never heard from again.

* * *

Martin Willius arrived from Germany around 1853 and made his way to Muskegon. Three years later he had found employment with Robert Jibson of Bridgeton Township and began working as a farm hand. At the same time he preempted his own land of 120 acres, which he later increased to 200 acres.

In 1866 he married Robert Jibson's daughter, Ann Elizabeth. She had just turned 16. Martin was 31. Though they had lost a son, John, early in their marriage, by 1876 they had five healthy, young girls.

Martin was doing well on the farm, raising winter wheat, Indian corn, and oats. He also maintained oxen, cattle, and swine. He continued to clear and improve his land for more farming.

But a great sadness once again crept through this woodland. Diphtheria came calling again. It is hard to imagine the panic that must have been at the heart of many a parent. Every sniffle, every flushed face from too much hard play, examined and prayed over; the nights of getting up to check the little ones while they slept.

The pervasive fear that came from neighbor visiting neighbor, or of going for supplies, must have entered into every decision to leave their

Chapter Nine: The Invisible Enemy

home. How could you protect yourself from something you could not even see? Perhaps an innocent person, who, as yet, did not have symptoms, would make contact with another. It only took one to infect many.

This disease did not discriminate, taking young and old alike. And it was fast.

The first to go was Ellen, age six, on November 17, 1881. Just fifty three days later, Ida, age five, succumbed to the disease; and, sadly, on the same day, their mother, Ann Elizabeth, only 31 years of age, also died of diphtheria.

How helpless the father and daughters must have felt knowing death was near and there was nothing they could do to stop it. Fear must have filled them for those who were, as yet, still healthy. The girls had lost their sisters and playmates; their nurturing mother. Martin lost his wife and helpmate. Now the girls, Anna 14, Mary 12, and Emma 9, were left to help their father run the farm and to take care of each other as best they could.

All three daughters survived and lived out their lives in the Sitka area. Anna became Mrs. Adolph Freudenstein, Emma married Algott Johnson, and Mary became the wife of Henry E. Zerlaut, living out her life in the original home of Henry and Adelia.

* * *

In the spring of 1879 Laura Matthews, who had marveled at her idyllic life where 'wild deer grazed in the meadows', was anxiously awaiting the birth of another child. The baby, due to be born in August, would be child number four for this couple. She was happy the long winter was over and now springtime was upon them; it was the time of new beginnings. She busied herself taking care of sons, Freddy and Willie, and their daughter, Lillie.

But soon these lives would be shattered. Scarlet fever rolled through the woodland, like an ugly squall, consuming all in its path. Nowhere was it safe. Though all precautions were taken—the school closed, families stayed in their homes, praying the disease would pass them by—the Matthews family was still hit, and hit hard.

It began with Freddie. At only six years old, he died on May 1. The grief-stricken parents could barely withstand the shock, when just three days later another devastating blow hit them. On May 4 both Willie, age four, and toddler, Lily Belle, just one year old, were taken. Fred and Laura had lost their entire family in just seventy-two hours!

One wonders how anyone could go on from such a loss. Laura herself wrote that she was 'broken in health and spirits'. Once the cabin had been full of rambunctious laughter of little children; now there was just deadly quiet. Once a table was set for a family of five; now three empty places faced them. Piles of little clothes and their few playthings lay untouched. The routine of the family in their little cabin was gone forever. Yet, somehow Laura had to go on. She had to prepare for the new baby, due in just a few weeks.

There must have been great hope for this birth; the promise of another child to love and nurture. It was not to be. Jesse was born August 16 and died a few months later.

I was honored, a short time ago, to be taken by a member of the Matthews' family, to the little cemetery in the woods on the ancestral farm, where these children are buried. It was a beautiful day in May, maybe not unlike the days in May when these children died. The sun was shining, the birds carrying on in song, and wildflowers bursting out in bloom. After 137 years the Matthews' family still lovingly cares for their graves. A wooden fence surrounds four headstones with the names Freddie, Willie, Lily Belle, and Jesse. Looking at these little graves, it is impossible to not be moved by the loss this family suffered.

After their tragedy, many in the community were shocked and

terrified, as one can imagine. Laura wrote that even the circuit preacher, Rev. Bacon, who had worked 'with zeal and determination' in the area, upon hearing of 'an epidemic of scarlet fever broke out at Sitka, the poor man was so frightened he ever after gave Sitka a wide birth.'

Laura and Fred, though the memory of their children was ever with them, were later blessed with two more children. Mary was born in 1882, and George in 1886; thankfully, both lived into adulthood.

* * *

The epidemics were so pervasive hardly a family was left untouched. Bereaved families covered the landscape where ever one looked. The three Crawford brothers lost their mother Lydia, and sisters Ann and Martha. Newcomer James Trumbull, also a Civil War veteran, and wife, Ellen, lost their thirteen year old child. Henry Wilde rests in the family cemetery with six children. Only a few of their headstones have dates, but those that do speak of a time of epidemics.

As the community neared the turn of the century they pulled together. Such devastating losses are hard to overcome, but once more they proved just how resilient they were.

Chapter Ten

A Town in the Making

Many people began to seize the opportunities that population growth could offer. The area now had two school buildings for the children that were also used for community and church gatherings; but there were other needs as well.

In 1885 McCager Sherman opened a blacksmith shop. Shortly after, Vicki and George Rainourd secured goods and resold them from their home on the present day Dezinski property. Shopping at their store could save a day long journey to Fremont to buy staples such as tea and coffee, sugar, salt, and molasses. Four years later, in 1892, Robert Shiffert bought out the Rainourd's store and began his own business. Fayette Crawford had a store on the Holly Crawford property close to where the community hall now stands. In 1892 he moved the store building to the Jibson farm and sold the vacant land to Joseph Zerlaut Jr. Joseph built a two story building there to be used as a store, community hall, and post office. A blacksmith shop was located nearby.

The Sitka post office, which began in 1868 in the home of Holly Crawford, was closed in 1885, but reopened in 1891 with Holly Crawford again as postmaster. Mail was brought from Holton to the Sitka post office by the Badeaux family. In 1893 Joseph Zerlaut Jr. took over the postmaster duties until the post office was permanently closed in 1901 with the establishment of rural free delivery. At that time, Hans Sorenson and Frank Bacon, the first mail carriers, covered two rural routes serving 200 people in the Sitka area.

The future looked bright again for this community. There was room for even more growth for those who wished to open their own business, continue to farm, or as many did, do both at the same time. They had survived hardships, but with perseverance and hard work, they could see

Chapter Ten: A Town in the Making

their efforts begin to pay off. But for some, a new tragedy would slow progress.

Between one and two p.m., Thursday, June 12, 1902, the sky over Sitka grew exceedingly dark. Unknown to the inhabitants, a severe storm had just passed over Holton with high winds, hail, and lightning. As it passed, the storm split with half the storm moving over Cedar Creek doing considerable damage. The other half had Sitka in its sights.

It first touched down two miles west of Sitka and continued its path of destruction for over four miles to the home of Frank Tietsort. Roads were left nearly impassable by uprooted trees, limbs, and other debris. Fences were demolished and buildings damaged or destroyed. Shingles were ripped from roofs, chimneys taken down, and barns flattened.

According to the Muskegon Daily Chronicle, Mrs. Madison, wife of the proprietor of the Sitka store, was alone with her three young children. Mr. Madison was out with his wagon four miles away. Mr. Lewis, who owned the black smith shop nearby, was standing outside watching the storm approach.

One of the Madison boys ran out, grabbed the hand of Mr. Lewis, and urged him to come into the store, but he refused. He said he would stay and watch it and if the wind got too strong he would just grab hold of an old safe that was sitting on a platform nearby. Mrs. Madison then went out and prevailed upon Mr. Lewis to take shelter with them, but again he refused. The last she saw of him he was hanging on to a plow.

No sooner had Mrs. Madison returned to her children in the store than the tornado reached the building, first moving it several feet, then causing its complete collapse. Mrs. Madison's two sons were not injured and were soon able to crawl out and summon help. Mrs. Madison, who had been knocked out by flying debris, was under a pile of rubble with only her hands visible. She was soon rescued and found to be not seriously injured. Her daughter suffered cuts and bruises about the head, but was otherwise unhurt. It was then that Mr. Lewis was missed. An active search soon found his crushed, unrecognizable body in the ruins. In looking at photos of the destruction, it is amazing that Mr. Lewis was the storm's only fatality. He was 61 years old and had moved to the area only two years previously.

Though the residents were surely overcome by the material losses and the sudden death of Mr. Lewis, there was one resident who saw things in a different light. In her writings about the beginnings of the Sitka church, Laura Matthews writes about the August revival held in 1901 in an area of the store that was often used for church services. Speaking of the tornado that hit the following June, she wrote, 'the Sitka hall where meetings were held was destroyed by a cyclone. I verily believe it was the vile uses to which this building was put after being hallowed by these services that brought God's judgement.' Though no specifics on the vileness is mentioned, it has been rumored that this place was also used as a house of prostitution! Whatever it was, Laura felt God's 'house' had been vindicated.

After the storm, people began picking up the pieces and rebuilding. The Madisons retrieved as many undamaged store goods as they could find. They moved these goods to their residence and operated from there until the owner, Joseph Zerlaut, could rebuild. Joseph completed a new two story building in 1903. The east half was used as a general store. The rest of the building was a community hall where the Grangers met and church services were conducted. In 1904 Joseph married Elizabeth Houlding and moved to her parent's farm in Ashland Township, leaving the Sitka area for good.

Eventually other businesses were attached to the store. There was a feed mill operated by George Start and a successful creamery that once bragged of taking in 4000 pounds of cream in one week! The store owner made frequent trips to Muskegon to sell cream, eggs, and butter. The Sitka news in the Fremont paper often commented on shipments for the store, such as 'Gold medal flour sitting on the tracks' in Holton waiting to be picked up, a car load of salt, new spring dry goods, or the arrival of a new supply of poultry food sure to increase egg production.

The store became the central gathering place for the neighbors, where gossip could be exchanged, weather and crops discussed, and community gatherings planned. Early photos show many horse drawn wagons and buggies pulled up front on a decidedly rough dirt road.

The store went through numerous owners over the years. Other names attached to the store were: Frank Stillwell, McCormick, Ezra Reames, George Vanschoten, John Wilson, Nelson Osborn, George Start, Fred Timmer, Isaac Wolbrink, and Matthew Glasen, who closed the store permanently in June 1957. Fourteen years later the building was torn down and no sign of the once thriving business remains.

Chapter Eleven

Bands and Baseball

Despite all the hardships over the years, the people of Sitka had a yearning for fun. Music often played an important role.

The Sitka Marching Band was formed by Fayette Crawford as the director in 1892. There were sixteen members who performed in elaborate dress band uniforms and hats. The instruments were mostly various types of horns, but there were drums as well. They would gather to practice each week and performed at various activities in the area. When they had to go far from home, they used two teams of horses hitched to a band wagon with benches along each side.

When I was growing up, the uniform, hat, and horn belonging to my grandfather, Henry Zerlaut, was stored in a closet on the second floor of our home. As kids we attempted to play the horn and tried on the uniform. It was very heavy and must have been horribly hot in the summer.

That these men from so many diverse backgrounds could come together in their busy lives with their various musical talents to form such a band is quite amazing. I was unable to find out just how long the band was in existence, but the names of fifteen of the members are known. They were: Fayette Crawford (director), Guy Crawford, Jay Crawford, Perrin Crawford, Ruben Crawford, Martin Jibson, Prince Jibson, Tom Jibson, Fred Ruggles, Fred Wilde, William Young, Frank Zerlaut, George Zerlaut, Henry Zerlaut, and Joseph Zerlaut Jr.

Another musical activity was held at the dance hall, also called the bowery, which was located on property belonging to the Trumbull family, across from the Henry Zerlaut home. It was an open structure sporting only a roof over a wooden floor. Many a lively dance was held there in the summer with music from area residents. Two fiddlers in the area,

Robert McKie and Frank Fritz, would have provided foot tapping music. The bowery was eventually moved, as my father remembered, by being jacked up on logs and rolled through the fields to a new location near the corner of 104th and Maple Island Road.

Almost any activity seemed to call for a musical celebration, so barn raisings, house parties, box socials and other events would bring the community together to dance or just listen to good music. This continued for many years, especially after the Sitka hall was built in 1903. Music gave these hard working people something to look forward to after a long day's work and brought the community closer together.

But, not to be outdone, some residents were more inclined to another type of physical activity. Around 1901 a baseball team called the Sitka Independents was organized. Due to a fire which destroyed all copies of the Fremont newspaper from 1880 to 1912, much information has been lost about this team. Later newspapers relate how very supportive the community was, not only by watching the games, but also with their wallets. Twice there were fund raisers for the team held at the Sitka hall. Money was donated to buy the team the Sitka team shirts they wore. In the newspaper dated April 16, 1935, a dance was announced to be held at the hall Saturday evening for the benefit of the Sitka ball team. A year later another dance was held which was attended by 'a very large crowd.' The news mentioned the team at various times between 1922 and 1937. Oh, how I wish we could see the missing newspapers, but it is clear this was a very active team for a long time. One can imagine the community gathering to watch them practice or play on the north east corner of Sitka across from the store, where a few years later Harold Zerlaut would plant his cherry orchard. People from the community would often gather to travel to 'away' games to support the team.

The names of many teams were mentioned which seemed to play each other on a regular basis. Besides the Sitka Independents, there were The Holton All Stars, Dalton Grange, Colored Giants of Muskegon, Scott's Grocery, Walkerville CCC, Muskegon Hoosiers, PNA of Muskegon,

Peterman's Sport Shop of Muskegon, and teams from Fremont, Maple Island, and Dayton Center.

Over the years there were many different team members, but an existing photo of the team, year unknown, shows the following players: Frank Carr, Wiley Tietsort, Pearl Buck, Arnt Meyers, Ernie Jensen, Raymond Kempf, Roy Tietsort, Walter Hanson, and Charlie Kempf.

The following two excerpts are from the Sitka Community News as they appeared in the Fremont Times Indicator.

> The Sitka Independents won a hard fought game from the fast P.N.A. of Muskegon, Sunday at Maple Island. C. Matthews who starred for the winners was injured in the 6th inning, but stayed in the game, although he wobbled in the 7th, and allowed 2 hits and 4 passes, which accounted for 3 runs for the P.N.A. giving them a 7 to 6 score. But in the 8th and 9th, he was very effective. In the 9th, with 2 outs and bases loaded, Matthews slammed out a clean two-base hit, which scored 3 runs that won the game for Sitka. Batteries: for Sitka, C. Matthews and T. Gibson, P.N.A., S. Felcoski and Halasinski. (September 3, 1936)

> After losing a close contest with the Walkerville CCC colored team Aug. 23 at Maple Island by a score of 6 to 5 in 10 innings, the Sitka team motored to Bitely Sunday and won the game by a score of 8 to 6 over the colored CCC's. Batteries for Sitka: Matthews and Gibson. Batteries for the CCC's: Hadden and Howe. Sitka collected 17 hits. CCC boys 9 hits. This being the last game of the season, after winning 8 games, and one claimed by default from Peterman's Sport Shop of Muskegon and lost 6 games. The boys had a very enjoyable time during this season with John Gustafson as manager and they are looking forward to a much faster team for 1937. (September 10, 1936)

In June 1937 the Sitka Independents beat the Muskegon Hoosiers 9 to 0 at Maple Island. They were off to a good season. Sadly, no more baseball games were reported in the paper.

Chapter Twelve
Sitka Grange Hall No. 861

By the early 1900s the seeds of community had been well planted and tended. The implementation of the Grange seemed to be the catalyst for the harvest.

The National Grange is the oldest agricultural organization serving rural America. It began in 1867 in Washington D.C. with the purpose of preserving and expanding American democracy. It was one of the first groups to allow women membership on an equal basis with men. Today it still promotes a better life for rural Americans, supporting stewardship of natural resources, rural education, improved road systems, rural communication, and medical services in rural areas. It also supports safe and properly labeled food products, cooperatives, and a competitive farm system.

In Sitka, the Grange began in the home of Holly Crawford in 1899. They were given an official charter on July 2, 1900 and became Sitka Grange No. 861. When Joseph Zerlaut Jr. built the store building in 1901, half of the building was reserved for community use. The Grange began meeting there until the cyclone of June 12, 1902 destroyed the building, along with the original Grange charter. A duplicate charter was issued July 1, 1902. This framed charter still exists today.

Rather than return to the store for meetings when it was rebuilt, it was decided to take out a loan and build their own structure. In 1903 Sitka Grange Hall No. 861 was built on property belonging to Holly Crawford. In 1911 Mr. Crawford deeded the property to the Grange.

It is not known how long the Sitka Grange existed. Due to a major fire at the state headquarters, many records were lost. It would appear, however, that they were active for nearly thirty years, as the Fremont paper often comments on their activities into the late 1930s. When it ceased to be used as a Grange hall the property reverted back to the Holly Crawford family. In 1945 Alethea M. Crawford and other family members deeded the property to the Sitka Community Club for one dollar.

The Grange was both a social and an educational entity. Though the group often met among themselves, more often than not they were joined by other local granges. Hosting these meetings gave local members great pride. Usually they were day long meetings filled with musical entertainment, recitations, educational lectures, and discussions of local concerns. As always, food was front and center during the mid-day break.

The meetings followed a fairly strict agenda which began with a roll call. However, they seemed to enjoy giving this a special twist. For example, in February of 1915 each member had to respond to roll call by giving a quotation from Longfellow. (One certainly hopes they had some advanced warning!) This was followed by a discussion on milk production.

Another time members were asked to respond to roll call with a recipe. Or being called upon, they were asked for suggestions on making their homes and the community more attractive.

The topics for lectures and discussions covered a wide range, with a particular focus on their goals for education and improvement of their community. Topics included:

> The care of young chickens
> What are the most durable farm fences?
> How to improve our schools
> At what cost 'sanitary milk' production?
> What are important needs of a successful fruit grower?
> What kinds of poultry are the most profitable?
> Should agricultural training be taught in public schools?
> What lessons have been learned from the World War?
> What influence will industrialism and commercialism have upon agriculture?
> How shall we provide rural children education opportunity equal to those offered to city children?

And this one got my attention:
Is there any reason why farm women should have an allowance?
(Audio recordings would be priceless!)

The hall itself was often used for purposes other than Grange meetings. The community at large made use of these premises on a routine basis for a whole variety of celebrations. Both the Jibson and Kempf schools made use of the building for Patron's Day celebrations, as well as 8th grade graduations. Here is where they shared their yearly school Christmas programs, called 'The Christmas Tree'. The community also held New Year's Eve parties, St. Patrick Day dances, and Halloween socials at the Grange hall.

In 1915 a 4th of July celebration with a basket picnic was held with the 'customary appendages of ice cream and fire crackers. Red lemonade, too. Roller skating afternoon and evening. Everyone welcome. Russel Crawford has recently purchased the roller skates from the Gardenour boys and has repaired the old skates and purchased a lot of new ones so as to be ready for the Fourth.' (Fremont Times Indicator, July 1, 1915)

In March of 1914 the boys of the neighborhood spent considerable time sanding down the floors in the hall to prepare for roller skating parties. The 'rink' opened in June with a very good attendance. In fact, so well, that it was decided to open for skating every Wednesday and every other Friday and Saturday evening. More skates had to be ordered to provide for all who wanted to skate. A small charge was made for those who brought their own skates or a rental fee for those without them. It was later decided to serve ice cream on skating nights.

My father was only fifteen when roller skating was organized. When asked about it, he said he had tried it, but did not much like the feel of wheels on his feet.

There was plenty going on for the adults as well. Card parties, in particular pedro and bunco, were often followed with dancing and supper at midnight. Masquerade dances and 'old time dress' parties were popular.

Violins, piano, and drums provided the music.

Outside groups were often brought in to provide entertainment. A group from Muskegon presented one of many plays called 'A Southern Cinderella.' Admission: 15 cents and 25 cents. A performance by the Clodhoppers band was given in April 1928 with the following month promising 'good snappy music'.

Dancing, games and entertainment were provided to honor Rose Lehman upon returning from Detroit for a visit. One hundred guests attended a farewell party for the J. E. Wilson family. Eighty people attended a welcome to the new store owners, Mr. and Mrs. Wolbrink, and a 25th wedding anniversary party was well attended for Mr. and Mrs. Raymond Kempf. Over the years countless birthdays, weddings, anniversaries, and reunions have taken place at the Sitka hall.

A hall is a good place for fund raisers. In 1922 a fund raiser was held to buy a piano for the hall. The baseball team profited from a gathering to buy new team shirts. The Ladies Aid Society held many fund raisers, one collecting $45 towards the pastor's salary. The schools frequently used the hall as a place to raise money as is shown in the following from 1927:

> The Kempf and Jibson schools are giving a box social and Halloween entertainment Saturday evening, Oct. 29, at the Sitka Hall. The frolic will begin at 7:30 standard time and the proceeds will be used to apply on a Victrola and records. The ladies are asked to bring boxes. Bring your friends and have a good time. (Fremont Times Indicator, October 27, 1927)

Later, the Jibson School performed a play called 'Wild Ginger'. The hall was packed and another $37 was taken in.

The hall was a place for meetings to be held when concerns of the community had to be discussed, such as the 1915 meeting to learn about the possibility of phone lines coming from Fremont to the area.

The large open space of the hall allowed for projects of a bigger magnitude to be accomplished. In 1913 the Ladies Aid Society met there to tie 'comfortables' they had made during the year. These quilts were sold and the money was used for church work. In 1938 the women of the community met to sew materials for the Red Cross. And in 1941 the Mattress project took pace. There were several of these projects in and around the area. The women gathered to sew tick mattresses for the needy. Nine hundred and thirty mattresses were made in the county. The mattresses were given to families with low incomes.

The people of Sitka knew how to work hard and play hard. No matter the reason for gathering one thing was for certain, it would invariably have music and food attached to it. This was especially seen in the socials.

There were so many socials! Pie socials—the women brought the pies, the men brought the money. Ice cream, egg, and box socials. Shadow socials—the women brought dinner for two and the men 'bought' the shadows. Oyster dinners, chicken pie suppers, and sauerkraut and frankfurters were popular menu items. Spring would bring maple syrup and hot biscuits, soon followed by raspberry shortcake socials. These people loved to eat.

The decision to build the hall in 1903 certainly turned out to be beneficial. It brought the people together in so many different ways, strengthening the community, and reaffirming their choices of making Sitka their home. They had, it seemed, arrived. They had the Grange hall, a store, blacksmith shop, creamery, mill, post office (recently closed), two schools, a band and dance floor, and even their own baseball team! What more could they want? But there was still one element missing that helped to build a rural community. There was still no church!

Chapter Thirteen

The Little Church with the Big Heart

In the early years of the Sitka settlement everything of importance was done in the homes of the people. The Rainourd's grocery sold precious food staples from their home, children were schooled at the Sox's log cabin, and funerals were conducted in the homes of the deceased with burial on the family farm. But there was a yearning by the faithful for a spiritual home.

Much is owed to Laura Matthews for recording the early endeavors and final success of the Sitka Methodist Church in her document titled, 'A Brief Review of the Rise and Struggles and Success of the Methodist Episcopal Church of Holton and Sitka', written in 1917.

It began with D. W. Parsons who took an appointment in Holton in 1873 preaching from the home of Mr. and Mrs. Corvill. By 1874, due to his hard work and diligence, the Holton church was built and Laura and her husband, Fred, traveled the five and a half miles to attend services there. It was not an easy trip with horses on roads that were so often in poor condition.

In 1875 the first service was held in Sitka by Rev. Matthews. However, his stay in Sitka was very brief as he felt his services were worth $100 a year, but the people at the time felt this was too large a sum for them to contribute. Later, Rev. Lightwater attempted to hold services in Sitka, but left for the same reason. At a quarterly conference it was reported that Twin Lake and Holton had each paid the pastor one dollar for the quarter. No mention was made of Sitka. When the financial report was read, Rev. Russell, the Presiding Elder, was so shocked he stated, "I cannot understand how even a single man can live on that amount."

It was later learned that Rev. Lightwater had lived on crackers and cheese and whatever meals were offered by parish families he visited. The following year the proprietor of the hotel in Holton allowed him 21 meals for three dollars a month, which he paid for by working as a blacksmith. However, to save money he usually went without breakfast.

In 1877 Rev. J. T. Alcott began services in Sitka with better attendance and improved support of the community. Next, Rev. Bacon, full of passion and determination, came. He was successful in getting a small log building erected across from the Christopher Kempf farm which was dedicated on June 19, 1879. This building was later moved to the site of the Kempf school, across from Fred and Laura Matthew's home. 1879 was also the beginning of the diphtheria and scarlet fever epidemics that took the lives of so many Sitka residents. It wasn't long before Rev. Bacon, afraid of disease, fled the area never to return. In September 1879 Rev. George Varian came, but he, too, did not stay long.

What followed was a time of little church activity. Laura Matthews said that she 'being broken in health and spirits' let the work of the church go unattended. Who could blame her? She had lost all of her children to scarlet fever. Others of the neighborhood must have felt much the same way. The deaths of their loved ones were still very fresh in their memory. There were occasional services held by preachers of other denominations, Rev. Fleming and Rev. Wood of the Fremont United Brethren being the most remembered, but little else.

During the time between 1879 and 1901 a Sabbath School (held on Sundays) was organized with Guy Crawford as superintendent. This Sabbath School was held in the Kempf School, often called the brick school, because of its exterior. In 1901 Laura, her spirit rekindled, felt the need for something more at Sitka and approached the presiding elder at the Holton church to gain consent to once again try to establish a Methodist church in Sitka. So in the winter of 1901 a series of revivals were held in the west end of the Sitka store. After the August revival of 1901 Rev. Herring from Holton and Rev. Davis of Sand Lake were able to form the Sitka class with 14 members and 5 probationers. The members were: Fred and Laura Matthews, Charles Smith, Estella Matthews, Clara Smith, Albert and Blanche Haire, Mr. and Mrs. William Palmer, Mrs. M. Higbee, Effie Jibson, Sadie Jibson, Brace Smith and George Matthews. The probationers were usually younger people waiting to take membership classes. They were: Ella Bowers, George Crawford, J. B. and Lola Frizells and John Jibson.

It was in June of 1902 that a tornado destroyed the Sitka store, where community meetings and services were held in the west end of the building. Services after that were shuffled between the Jibson and Kempf schools. Laura became the Sabbath School superintendent and church services were conducted by Rev. J. L. Merahon, who was much loved, but had to resign due to health issues. Rev. Haskill, who greatly increased attendance, replaced him, but soon reached the age limit of the Michigan conference and was forced to retire.

After many attempts to hold services at either school by Rev. W. S. Phillips, they were discontinued for a time due to bad roads and poor attendance. Laura was finally able to gain permission of Mr. VanSchoton, proprietor of the rebuilt Sitka store, to hold services there. The Sabbath School flourished with an enrollment of 60 people. The Sabbath School was later reorganized into a Missionary School with a missionary program given the first Sunday of each month.

It was the arrival of Rev. W. H. H. Bunch in 1907 that led to the biggest change for the Sitka church community. With the congregation growing, he impressed upon them the importance of having their own building for church purposes. A meeting was called February 28, 1908 by Rev. Bunch and held in the home of Holly Crawford. Those who attended agreed to proceed with plans to build a Methodist Episcopal Church. They elected George Crawford, Fred Matthews, and Robert Kempf as trustees, with Guy Crawford as secretary-treasurer. Plans were selected and a subscription paper was written and circulated. Those present made a commitment of $475.

The subscription paper read as follows:

> We the undersigned agree to pay the sum set opposite our names to the trustees of the Methodist Episcopal Church in Sitka, Mich. for the purpose of erecting a Methodist Episcopal Church in the above named place. Said church to be known as the Sitka M. E. Church. Said building not to cost more than twelve hundred dollars. Said money to be paid as follows, unless otherwise agreed upon by the pastor concerned, one half on or before the day that the foundation is laid and the balance when the building is enclosed. It is further agreed that no subscription is valid until the lot is procured and eight hundred in cash is subscribed.

Later subscribers brought the total to $2,114.49, which covered the final costs of erecting and furnishing the church. For people who had earlier balked at paying a pastor $100 a year, they had come a long way. It was now official—they would soon have a church.

The land procured belonged to Hattie L. Jibson, wife of Prince Jibson, and her widowed father, James. W. Trumbull. For the sum of one dollar a half acre was secured by the trustees with express conditions that the property was to be used strictly for church purposes.

With the land in place, plans and specifications for the building were prepared by Cramer & son for a cost of ten Dollars. These detailed architectural drawings showing every angle of the proposed building still exist and are currently on display at the Sitka United Methodist Church.

Once the plans were accepted a contractor needed to be hired. On June 20, 1908 Phillip Homer and Perrin Crawford agreed to erect the M. E. Church for $750. A few changes were made preceding the signing of the contract, one being that the trustees would do the excavation. Phillip Homer was to do the carpentry work and Perrin Crawford was to do the masonry work. It was estimated that 3000 cement blocks would be needed. These blocks were to be made on site by Mr. Crawford. Work on the church soon began.

My father, Harold Zerlaut, was nine years old at the time the church was built. He remembers seeing Perrin Crawford going by the house early in the morning on his motorcycle. He was on his way to Grand Rapids to check out a church there that the Sitka church was being patterned after to check out details.

But a church is more than cement blocks and a roof. Fifteen oak pews were purchased from Superior Manufacturing Co. in Muskegon for $190. A bell from M.W. and Co. was obtained for a cost of $29. The cornerstone of the church declaring its establishment in 1908 was purchased for seven dollars. An organ was provided thanks to the donation of funds from the Ladies Aide Society. Of course, there was a furnace that was needed and a variety of other materials. Considering where this community was thirty years prior, they were not holding back on making this the best possible church they could. Nothing they could afford seemed to be overlooked. By December of 1908, less than a year after that first meeting, the church was finished. A shed was provided for horses to be tied during services. Perrin Crawford and Phillip Homer were paid in full for their labors.

The church not only welcomed the people of the community, it seems it also offered fellowship for the Indians in the area. Many years later Guy Crawford reminisced on 'how the church invited Indians to the services in the early days. He pointed out recently how the Indians used to camp with their teepees in the woods south of 96th, between Dickinson and Maple Island Road, about one half mile west of the present church.' (Fremont Times Indicator, September 30, 1976) This was especially true during the season of collecting sap from the maple trees.

The church was dedicated December 17, 1908 by C. C. Chase, District Superintendent. Can you imagine the excitement of that first church service only six days before Christmas—the bell pealing out its call to the congregation, the hymns on the new organ, voices in song raised to the rafters, the thankful prayers, and the absolute joy of having accomplished their goal?

Chapter Fourteen
Supporting Organizations of the Church

At the same time as plans were being made for building the church, other groups were being formed that greatly influenced the Sitka congregation. On January 30, 1908 a gathering of women called a meeting to organize a Ladies Aid Society. The L.A.S was fairly new in the Methodist church, having only been recognized in 1903. The following month the by-laws were written and accepted. The object of the L.A.S was to promote the financial, social, and spiritual interest of the church. The group was open to any lady of good standing in the community. The monthly dues were ten cents and it was agreed to meet every two weeks. Any gentleman could become an honorary member by paying the sum of one dollar.

The original officers elected were Laura Matthews, president; Sadie Jibson, vice-president; Mae Crawford, secretary; and Bertha Crawford, treasurer. By June of that year they had fourteen members.

The meetings opened with the singing of hymns, followed by scripture study and prayer. The first order of business was to collect funds or donations of materials for making quilts, which the ladies worked on together at meetings. Over the years many of these quilts, also called 'comfortables', were made by the L.A.S and sold. The hall was used for many fund raising socials by the L.A.S. The money was used for the church, even helping to pay the salary of the pastor when needed—one chicken dinner and fair netted $45 for the pastor. A later chicken supper brought in $80 for the L.A.S. They used various methods of raising money such as at one meeting where the members were encouraged to bring aprons and fancy work to sell.

In 1915 the L.A.S was able to purchase new hymnals, which were probably much appreciated by the newly formed choir. Also at that time they purchased two dozen chairs for the church to go with the tables the men had made at a work bee.

Most meetings were held in the homes of members, but larger projects, such as finishing quilts, were done at the hall. They also met at the hall and the church for the purpose of cleaning.

Besides supporting the Sitka church they also took part in donations for other worthy purposes outside the community, as they did at a meeting requesting each member to bring a dozen eggs to fill a crate for the Methodist hospital in Kalamazoo.

But the meetings weren't all work. As their by-laws stated, it was also a social group, and socialize they did! Just reading about their various meetings you can almost hear the laughter.

The following reports are typical of what appeared in the Fremont Times Indicator concerning the activities of the Sitka Ladies Aid Society:

> The Sitka Ladies Aid society met with Mrs. N. H. Osborn last Wednesday. Over 40 were present and very enjoyable time was spent. Mrs. Rice favored the ladies with a very humorous reading, Mrs. Frank Zerlaut rendered a pleasing instrumental solo and Mesdames Ruggles, Guy Crawford and Fred Matthews sang. In a contest entitled 'The Work Basket', Mrs. Walter Hansen won the prize which was one ball of darning cotton. (October 9, 1913)
>
> Sitka Ladies Aid society met with Mrs. Osborn last Thursday and enjoyed a basket dinner of chicken, etc. After dinner the regular business session was held and Mrs. Elliott recited after which the ladies were handed slips of paper upon which they were requested to write the name of the article sold in a general store represented by pictures cut from magazines and pinned upon the wall. Mrs. Elliott won the prize guessing 17 out of 18 advertisements. The prize was a 10 cent package of Ralston Wheat Food. (March 9 1916)
>
> Sitka Ladies Aid society met with Mrs. John McKie last Wednesday afternoon. In spite of rain and mud there was a good attendance and the committee consisting of Mesdames John, Robt. and Chas. McKie and Mrs. Dagan, served a delicious fish supper. One new member was received. In a bean contest in which the contestants walked a chalk line and carried dry navy beans on a silver knife, Grandma McKie who is 85 years old was the victor as she succeeded in reaching the goal without losing a bean. (June 15, 1916)

Chapter Fourteen: Supporting Organizations of the Church

The L. A. S. met at John Jibson's last week. Owing to the stormy day there was not a large crowd out. As a feature of entertainment each member was provided with a piece of paper, a stick of gum and a toothpick with which each person was directed to make a black cat. The one who made the best cat was awarded a prize of a can of pumpkin. Mary Crampton was the lucky one. Refreshments of pumpkin pie, doughnuts and coffee were served. (November 2, 1916)

The Ladies Aid Society held a celebration of their 50th anniversary at the home of Mrs. Kenneth Nobel in December of 1960. A Christmas supper of chicken was served to 30 members. They reviewed their achievements of the past year; the most important being seven large boxes of clothing, collected, packed, and delivered to the Traverse City State Hospital for the patients. Also a needy child in Newaygo County was given $15 for clothing, continuing their pledge to service.

* * *

Two other groups soon emerged which were focused on the young people of the community. The young people of the church organized a Young People's Society of Christian Endeavor in 1914. Pastor Francis E. Clark of Maine began the organization in 1881 because he felt young people needed activities to challenge them. He wanted to better prepare them for service to God. The work eventually spread across the nation forming chapters within many different denominations.

Each meeting had a different young person as leader. At their first gathering they responded to roll call with a quotation from Longfellow, and then proceeded to study the poet. This was followed by several meetings centered on U. S. history with history contests at the end of the meetings. A study and discussion of the novella Silas Marner by George Elliot (Mary Anne Evans), was the focus of another meeting, where it was stated almost everyone present took part.

One of the most interesting meetings with Neva Zerlaut as leader was a debate on the woman's vote. The Fremont Times Indicator reported the meeting as follows:

> A good debate on the subject, 'Resolved that Woman Suffrage is Right in the U. S.' Affirmative Misses Birdie Miller, Stacia Donahue and Mrs. Mary Crampton. Negative, Louis Ruprecht, Jr., Harold Kempf and Russel Crawford. Judges appointed were Gilbert Kempf, Miss Canniff, of Fremont, and Neva Kempf who decided unanimously in favor of the affirmative. Afterwards Mr. Orla Miller related his own observations of Woman suffrage in California. He was in that state when Woman Suffrage carried. (Times Indicator, April 22, 1915)

Not surprisingly, Birdie Miller, Stacia Donahue and Neva Zerlaut were, or soon became, teachers in the area working at both the Kempf and Jibson schools.

The Young People's Society continued for many years with a large crowd for their annual Christmas banquet with entertainment at the hall in 1926. Though no further mention was made of their meetings, for many years these young people continued the Sitka tradition of education.

At nearly the same time many of the same young people formed the Epworth League in 1916. The Epworth League took its name from the birthplace of John and Charles Wesley. It was made up of individuals ages 18-35. Organized by the Methodist Episcopal Church in 1889, it had the purpose of promoting community, missions, and spiritual growth. Elected officers were George Crawford, Russel Crawford, Marion Jibson, Clara Hanson, Martin Rummelt, Dorothy Jibson and Sylva Buck.

This was also a social organization, as a gathering in May, 1916 suggests. After the meeting adjourned, a game of indoor baseball in the basement of the church was pursued.

In August, 1916 a new subscription paper was circulated to raise money for repairs on the Sitka church. The Epworth League donated $10. Originally the church was built with clear glass windowpanes. Now they were ready to replace these with stained glass. A committee made up of all parts of the church was formed. Rev. Elliot, Frank Zerlaut, and George Crawford represented the church, Mrs. F. Young and Mrs. H. Reams represented the L. A. S., and the Epworth League had Neva Kempf as their representative. They traveled to Muskegon together to order the new stained glass windows at a cost of eighty dollars. A month later the church windows were removed and hauled to Muskegon by Fred Young and Rev. Elliott. There the plain glass was exchanged for stained glass panels. One wonders how these precious windows were transported down uneven dirt roads by horse and wagon without damage for a distance of about twenty miles and reinstalled in the church. What an undertaking! But they were successful and all remarked on the beauty it brought to the little church.

The Epworth League arranged for a five part lecture series over the winter of 1916 to be held at the church. The first in the series was a talk by Rev. Russell Bready called 'Square with the World'. This was followed by Mrs. Laura Williams who gave a program of dramatic and humorous readings. The third in the series was a concert with piano, violin, and a reader. Next in the series was home talent. A play and vocal numbers were offered for the audience. Lastly, Rev. J. W. Esveld, of Fremont, gave a humorous and educational lecture called the 'The Sunny Side of Life'.

Tickets for these programs cost fifteen cents for children and twenty-five cents for adults. In order to make sure costs were covered, the Epworth League did what all the other organizations in Sitka did to raise money—they held socials! One pie social with music and recitations netted them twenty dollars. They often split the proceeds with the Ladies Aid Society.

Chapter Fifteen
Rallies, Revivals, and Temperance

Between 1914 and the early 1920s, rallies and revivals continued with many people flocking to the little community of Sitka.

One 1914 newspaper notice read: 'The pastor of the Sitka M. E. Church, Rev. R. Elliott, commenced revival meetings at Sitka church Monday night. Meetings will be held every evening except Saturday, at 7:30 o'clock. Good singing, inspiring services. Everybody welcome.' (Fremont Indicator, December 3, 1914) The church grew under the leadership of Rev. Elliott. He baptized a class of eleven in 1917 and a few weeks later baptized another class.

In 1914 many of the rallies began to center around the interests of the Anti-Saloon League, which was not surprising as it drew most of its support from the Protestant evangelical churches. The Anti-Saloon League was founded in 1893 and quickly grew. They had an ally in the Women's Christian Temperance Union, often referred to as W. C. T. U. Together they lobbied against the manufacture and sale of all intoxicating beverages.

The first speaker to come to the Sitka church was Mr. Rowden, an attorney from Ann Arbor. A short few months later the church was filled again to hear the address of another speaker. Grant H. Hudson of St. Johns held a service in 1918. People representing the league were willing to travel, sometimes great distances, to promote their message, and were met with large audiences at Sitka.

In 1919 the Eighteenth Amendment was adopted. Though the league fought for strict enforcement, the amendment was repealed in 1933 and interest in the Anti-Saloon league soon dwindled.

Another successful revival campaign, unrelated to temperance, was conducted at Sitka church in 1917. Rev. Elliott invited Rev. Jay J. Pease and his wife for a two week series of evangelistic meetings. Mrs. Pease was to lead the singing using the latest and best song books. Everyone who appreciated a good sermon was urged to attend. A large sum of money was contributed to their work at the end of the meetings.

Probably the most colorful person to conduct a rally at the Sitka church was Rev. Joe. J. Payne, known as the Cowboy Preacher. He held a series of meetings over a period of two weeks in September 1921, filling the church every time. One must consider how forceful these speakers were to sustain such crowds in a small community like Sitka.

Mr. Payne was 'born in a log hut in Texas, this house serving as the Methodist parsonage. His father and grandfather were ministers of the Methodist Church and served in the pioneer days of the great southern state. Joe was an active cowboy for seventeen years and served as a Texas Ranger for four years. He has seen much of the country and has been confronted with many and various problems of life.' (Fremont Indicator, October 31, 1923)

Mr. Payne traveled the world for several months with Buffalo Bill's Wild West Show and was part of another Wild West show called 101 Ranch. Shortly before coming to Sitka he was pastor of the White Cloud M. E. Church, but he left this position to work in the field of evangelism. Though he came dressed in cowboy attire—hat, boots, cowboy shirt, and gun belt (including pistols)—he was said to be charming, lacking in flamboyance, and a forceful speaker, drawing on his experiences as a cowboy. He chose the title, 'From Saddle to the Pulpit', for his meetings.

He received many glowing reviews in the Fremont Times Indicator. Consider the following:

> The cowboy is an unusually forceful and effective speaker. He has a fine physique, makes a splendid appearance, and talks straight from the shoulder. He has an excellent command of language, and a wealth of illustrations taken from his varied life as a cow puncher in the Lone Star state and on the road with the Wild West shows.

He delivers his sermons in plain understandable English and has the faculty of keeping his audiences in an expectant mood during his entire discourse. But there is nothing of the old type of shouting evangelism in the cowboy's preaching. He does not use any 'tricks' in forcing confessions from those in his congregations. He preaches the gospel truths in plain, effective language and makes his appeal through the logic of his arguments. (November 8, 1923)

Later in the year he addressed the M. E. Church of Fremont with one of the largest crowds ever gathered in that church with standing room only, leaving many outside unable to attend.

In the late 1920s the interest in large rallies seemed to have burned itself out, but what an interesting time it must have been when so many people were drawn to the little Sitka church.

These two images come from *A Pictorial Record of the Muskegon Lumbering Era* North Muskegon Historical Committee. Above: Ryerson-Hills Loggin Co., circa 1890. Below: a load of white pine.

After the timber was cut the stumps had to be removed. This is a lever or pulley type stump puller.

Portable saw mill

Anna Jibson

Robert Jibson

Early tractor, circa 1900

Cross of Lorraine

Elizabeth Steiner Zerlaut   Joseph Zerlaut

Trucky's Maple Island Trading Post

Family of Joseph and Anna Zerlaut

Joseph Zerlaut farm

Fred and Laura Matthews

Matthews Homestead

Jibson School 1883

Sitka Band uniform

Kempf School

Baseball team circa 1930s

Sitka marching band circa 1900

Wilde homestead, taken 2006

Sitka General Store circa 1920s

Sitka cyclone damage 1902

Frank Bacon, Fremont Rural Route No. 3 Mail Carrier - 1903

Holly Crawford Family

Former Sitka Grange Hall - this photo taken in 2006

Perrin Crawford, left, making cement blocks for Sitka Church - this photo taken in 1908

Sitka Church 1908

M. E. Church Sitka, Mich.

Charlie, Flora Carmichael and Oren Kempf

Cowboy Preacher Rev. Joe Payne

The threshing crew went from farm to farm during harvest in the Sitka area. This crew consists of, left to right: Albert Ruggles, Howard MacDonald, Brady Cottril, Robert Kempf, Doug MacDonald, Herman Zerlaut, Jake Hoffman, Gustav Kempf, Werner Kempf, Willie Fisher and the last person is unknown. This photo belonged to Werner and Mary Kempf.

Guy and Stella Crawford 1942

Sitka United Methodist Church - photo taken 2017

Sitka Hall - photo taken 2017

Community Hayride 2017

Community gathering at the hall 2017

Chapter Sixteen

The Church and the Schools

Before the church was built, services were held in various places—in homes, at the Jibson and Kempf schools, and at the store in the space reserved for meetings. So it is not surprising that when the M. E. Church was built the schools took advantage by using it for school activities. The church was well situated, being about equal distance between the two schools. The lines at that time between church and state were very blurred and no one gave this much thought.

Three main school events regularly took place at the church. The two schools held their 8th grade graduations together at the church. To receive a diploma the students first had to pass the county examinations. This done, the commencement exercises could take place. It was not uncommon for the diplomas to be given out by the local pastor. The Fremont Times Indicator reported one such graduation in 1917.

> Commencement exercises for the Kempf and Jisbon schools were held at the M. E. church in Sitka Friday evening, June 15, when a class of six pupils, three from each school, received eighth grade diplomas.
>
> The church was prettily decorated in the class colors of red, white, and blue. A novel and important feature of the program was a beautiful operetta given by twenty primary pupils from the Kempf School. Each child represented and acted the part of a flower which he or she carried.
>
> Rev. Magdanz, of Fremont, gave a thrilling address on 'Americanism and World-wide Democracy,' which was enjoyed and appreciated by a very large audience.
>
> Mr. Armantrout favored the audience with choice readings, and last but not least enjoyed was a duet sang by two small boys from the Kempf School.

The teachers, Miss Ruprecht and Mr. Armantrout, are to be congratulated upon their success. (Fremont Times Indicator, June 28, 1917)

After graduating 8th grade the students needed to make a decision about further education. Some, like my father and his sisters, boarded out during the school year in Fremont so they could attend high school. They would try to hitch rides back to Sitka for the weekend. It was not feasible to make a trip to Fremont every day to attend school. No means of transportation was available other than horse and buggy or a very few automobiles, which still had to travel often poorly maintained dirt roads.

Patrons' Day was another school related activity held regularly at the Sitka church. It was always an exciting time for the community. Former students and their families from both schools gathered at the church for a reunion.

> The annual Patrons' Day celebration was held at Sitka Wednesday, Mar. 15. Dinner was served in the basement of the church. Four long tables had been placed and were loaded with all sorts of good things to eat. First the children and teachers were served and afterwards the older ones. Nearly one hundred and fifty were present at dinner time and quite a few came to listen to the program who could not come to dinner. The children, as usual, did their parts well. The Jibson school having been closed for three weeks on account of scarlet fever, had very little time to prepare their parts and their teacher, Miss Donahue, is to be congratulated on the successful performance of her pupils. Of special interest was a pretty parasol drill by eight little girls of Miss Ruprecht's school and a Dutch Windmill song by little Vera Young in genuine Dutch costume, wooden shoes, and all, assisted by four little girls. Miss Carter, our county commissioner, was present and gave a good talk on 'School Ideals.' Miss Clara Hanson as editor of the local paper, gave some interesting items and Mrs. Carr, Mrs. Osborn and H. W. Zerlaut each gave short talks. Rev. Elliot gave a short address in his usual straightforward manner. Frank Nash, who ought to be above such things, took the house down with his rusty hoe and George Crawford's inability to leave off fishing. The day was beautiful and it is the general feeling that we had the best

Chapter Sixteen: The Church and the Schools

Patrons' Day ever. (Fremont Times Indicator, March 23, 1916)

'The Christmas Tree' was another event that took place each year, and was always called by that name, even into the 1950s and 60s when I attended the Jibson School. It was a celebration of Christmas for the students and their families. Much work was put into the performance that was to be given for the parents, which was similar to what they did for the Patrons' Day celebrations. Students would sing, give recitations, play instrumental music, or present a play. Reports of two such celebrations, one ending in near disaster, are given below.

> A large crowd attended the Christmas tree at Sitka church Christmas eve. A good program was enjoyed. A near accident occurred when Santa Claus whiskers caught fire. Fortunately the fire was immediately extinguished and nobody lost their wits so no real damage was done. (Fremont Times Indicator, December 31, 1913)

> The Christmas exercises at the church were a great success. Miss Ruprecht and Miss Donahue certainly may feel proud of their schools. The church was crowded to its utmost capacity and every feature of the program was carried out to perfection. The little folks were certainly well drilled in their parts and everyone was happy. (Fremont Times Indicator, December 30, 1915)

The use of the church for such activities appears to have ended in the mid-1920s when they were moved to the hall. By the time I attended grade school, 'The Christmas Tree' program was held separately at each individual school.

Though not directly related to the Sitka church, it is worth mentioning the Rural Bible Mission. The R. B. M. was incorporated in Michigan in 1944 with the goal of helping local churches, using the Word of God to shape the souls of the children in the rural areas. In the 1950s and 60s two wonderful ladies named Miss Arnold and Miss Enszer came to the Jibson school and other rural schools in the county. They came armed with the makings of a flannel board Bible story and were excellent story-tellers.

Each of us kept a card with bible verses in our desks, one for each month they came, which we were to memorize. They would start each visit by having us say the verses. Doing so correctly got you a 'punch' on your card alongside the verse. But not to worry, if you could not remember you always got a second chance after everyone else had finished. If by then you could not recite it, then you just weren't listening! We looked forward to their visits. It was a nice break in the routine.

Chapter Seventeen

Pandemic and War

About 80 people were present at the special service held in the Sitka church last Sunday, when a service flag was dedicated in honor of the young men of the community who are in the nation's service. Nine stars were placed on the flag for the following boys: Segt. Henry E. Ruggles, Fred R. Sherman, Russell Crawford, Lynn Crawford, Edwin Sharp, Harold Zerlaut, Christopher Kempf, Russel Ruprecht and Benjamin Paulson. Each one of the boys was represented by some member of the family being at the service. The pastor, Rev. A. R. Elliott, gave an address in which he spoke of the spirit and war practices of the Prussian military leaders, and outlined some of the ways in which we can all help to win the war. An impressive feature of the service was when the entire congregation marched past the platform and saluted Old Glory and also the Service flag. In the line was J. B. Ruggles, a veteran of the Civil war who has one son and three grandsons in the present war. (Fremont Times Indicator, March 21, 1918)

To find John Benjamin Ruggles singled out for mention in the paper is not surprising. He had served in the Seventh Connecticut Volunteers. He and his wife came to Sitka in 1881. He was always proud of his service in the Civil War. Each Memorial Day he would put on his uniform, hitch his horses to the hay wagon, and drive to Holton to be part of the Memorial Day Parade. By 1918 he would have been one of the last surviving Civil War veterans in the area.

On April 6, 1917, the United States entered into war. By the time it ended on November 11, 1918, nearly ten million people were killed and twenty million wounded, in what we now call World War I. For the young men of Sitka, many of whom had never been out of the county, let alone the country, the scope of what they were to be a part of must have been far beyond their imagination.

As they crisscrossed the nation in preparation for future deployment they wrote many letters home. These resembled vacation postcards in their enthusiasm for sights seen along the way. Comments, for instance, included: We are 'going up the mountains and I never saw such beautiful scenery.' And, we had a 'view of the Washington Monument from the train.' Once they were deployed overseas they continued commenting on their surroundings. They eagerly took in everything around them, not only describing the landscape, but the people, their homes, methods of farming, local food, and customs—and they had an opinion about everything.

Russel Crawford, stationed in France, found like many others, the language to be a bit of a challenge. 'I am pretty nearly lost over here where everybody speaks French except the rest of the boys. I am getting so I can understand it pretty well now though, and talk it some too, enough so I can ask for bread or coffee or go to the store and buy some toilet soap or to the laundry and get my clothes.' (Fremont Times Indicator, March 14, 1918)

Recently among my father's belongings he had saved from WWI, a booklet was found that he received from the Army Y.M.C.A. at Wilbur Wright Aviation Field in Dayton, Ohio called 'The Soldiers' French Phrase Book'. It stated that 'In the hope that it may prove a convenient and serviceable aid to the intelligible expression in French of words and phrases necessary to communicate the common wants, wishes and desires of everyday military and social life, this French Phrase Book is presented to the solider boys of America.'

Many vocabulary words were listed as well as common phrases or questions such as, 'Do you speak English? (Parlez-vous anglais)' and 'What time is it? (Quelle heure est-il?)' It contained the calendars for the years 1917 and 1918. Also included were the words of the Star-Spangled Banner and The Battle Hymn of the Republic. With all these new experiences, if it had not been for the war going on around them, this would have been a great adventure.

One thing they would not write about was the grisly side of the war.

Often they were not allowed to give their exact location; for example 'Somewhere in France' might be the only clue of their whereabouts. They were instructed to keep their letters positive so as not to worry families back home. So they wrote about camp life, living in the close quarters of tents or barracks, or life aboard ships and submarines. They told of hours of drills, hiking for miles, the camp food, how they had gained weight and were healthy, or the boredom of waiting for action of some kind. (Cf. Susan King, Letters Home, 2013). To get real news of the war people back home needed to read the newspapers.

Though letters were often censored, at times something a bit more specific might be shared. One soldier told how he practiced putting on gas masks in six seconds. Another related how he had just completed a course in 'Grenade and Bomb construction'. But for the most part they wrote folksy letters about daily life and sometimes even added a bit of humor, as did Lee A. Somers when he wrote that he could 'enjoy life now that they had stopped inoculating me.' (Fremont Times Indicator, May 16, 1918)

They could not say enough good things about the Y. M. C. A. and the Red Cross. While crossing the United States the Red Cross would meet the trains handing out oranges, cigarettes, hot coffee, sandwiches, and even ice cream cones. Most importantly they handed the men newspapers and stamped post cards so they could write home, which the Red Cross later mailed for them. They continued providing support once they were overseas, even doing the difficult job of notifying family members when a loved one was killed.

Representatives from the Y.M.C.A. rode the trains with them, singing and spending time talking with the men. Overseas they furnished places for them to go when not on duty. They provided entertainment almost every night, a speaker on Sunday, and gave them paper, envelopes, books, magazines and newspapers.

Back in Sitka, many more men had left for service since that first patriotic rally at the church. They continued holding patriotic rallies and at other church gatherings they often set aside a time for singing patriotic songs. The newspapers were full of news of the war.

The Ladies Aid Society met with the Red Cross Auxiliary from Grant in August of 1917 for a demonstration of Red Cross work. A month later Sitka had a Red Cross Auxiliary of their own. They met to do Red Cross work, though the type of work was never defined in the community news. The Red Cross sewing division supplied hospital bed shirts, pillow cases, sheets, handkerchiefs, tray cloths, napkins, bed socks, nightingales, pajama suits, and robes. These would be gathered from the various auxiliaries and shipped to Chicago and then on to Washington for dispersal. It is likely this is the type of work the Sitka auxiliary did.

This plea for the Red Cross was sent out by Albert E. Sleeper, governor of Michigan, just before Christmas, 1917. 'It is a privilege to call your attention to the Christmas Membership Campaign inaugurated by the Red Cross...There are five million members of the Red Cross in our country—it needs fifteen million to carry out its work... (I) call upon all our people to lend their assistance thereto by becoming members or renewing their memberships and by enrolling others in the organization.' (Fremont Times Indicator, December 20, 1917)

People were also encouraged to buy War Savings Stamps. The notice in the Fremont Times Indicator for a National War Savings Day proclaimed:

> Paste him in the eye with a War Savings Stamp—then paste him again and again. Don't think that you have already done your duty. Pershing's men 'over there' don't go home after their first battle—
> they go after the Huns again–they keep on pasting the Kaiser.
> Your government has officially set Friday, June 28th, National War Savings Day. On that day every American is summoned to 'sign the Pledge'–to save and invest in a definite amount of War Savings Stamps each month. Every real American will prove his patriotism by agreeing to regularly paste the Kaiser. (Fremont Times Indicator, June 20, 1918)

Chapter Seventeen: Pandemic and War

It is of interest to note that War Savings Stamps bought for $4.17 in 1918 would be worth $5.00 when they reached maturity on January 1, 1923. The gain in value of War Savings Stamps over the five year period was good news for locals, who bought the War Savings Stamps in abundance. It is reported, for instance, that in May, 1918 Newaygo County exceeded its quota for selling war bonds.

> Newaygo county's response to the Liberty Loan call is especially gratifying when the financial conditions of the rural citizens is considered. The farmers of this county have never experienced as unproductive a season as that of 1917. They certainly had no share in the 'war prosperity' of the past year. Yet their response was far more generous than in the first and second drives.' (Fremont Times Indicator, October 24, 1918.)

By spring 1918 it became necessary to reduce wheat consumption by one-half in order to feed our servicemen. This meant a ration per person amounted to 1 ½ pounds of wheat products weekly. The newspaper began printing recipes using barley, oatmeal, rice, buckwheat, and cornmeal as substitutes for wheat. This was followed by a call to have at least one meatless meal per week. Americans were also limited by sugar rations, which amounted to one-half pound per week per family, to ensure sugar could be sent to France.

The people of Sitka responded as we might expect. They cut back wherever they could.

> The Sitka Sunday school will go to Holton next Sunday afternoon to unite with the Holton school in the Union Children's Day Program which has become an annual feature with the two schools. The community dinner will not be given this year on account of the great demand for food conservation owing to the war. (Fremont Times Indicator, June 13, 1918)

> Sitka church surprised their pastor, Rev. A. R. Elliott and family, by bringing well filled baskets at noon and enjoyed a regular church family dinner together. The day being fine, tables were arranged under the trees on Osborn's lawn and nearly a hundred sat down together. Cake and pie were taboo except a big pumpkin pie, made from corn

syrup, for the preacher himself, who by the way, like all preachers, is found of pie. This completes Mr. Elliott' fourth year as pastor of this charge. (Fremont Times Indicator, September 12, 1918)

* * *

The close quarters of barracks, ships, and submarines became the perfect breeding grounds for many diseases. Many men never left the United States before they were hit with a variety of illnesses. Some wrote of being quarantined for twenty one days due to an outbreak of scarlet fever. My father had the misfortune of being inflicted with the mumps. But the unintended spread of the Spanish flu was the most devastating.

No one knows for sure where the Spanish flu began, but best documentation says it started at Fort Riley, Kansas. It was extremely contagious, moving through the camp and eventually killing 46 people. Soon many other camps around the U. S. were dealing with this deadly flu. Men leaving on transport ships took the flu with them to France, inflicting many, and soon the disease had traveled around Europe. Spain was the first country to publicly address the flu, thus the title 'Spanish' flu.

This deadly strain was different than previous ones. Instead of mostly attacking the very young or elderly, it seemed to target the young and healthy. Some patients died within hours. Hospitals were overwhelmed. There were not enough doctors as many had been sent to war. Bodies piled up. Sometimes mass graves had to be dug. Between September and November of 1918 as many soldiers were killed by the flu as were killed in war related deaths.

Back home the residents of Sitka began feeling the effects of the flu in November, 1918, which put a huge dampener on celebrations of the signing of the armistice on November 11. The outbreak of flu was coupled with several rounds of scarlet fever and mumps. Often pneumonia followed close behind. For those who had survived the scarlet fever and diphtheria epidemics of 1879, this must have been a horrible reminder of what wide-spread illness can do.

To add to the stress the winter of 1918-19 was one of the worst in years. Severe blizzards kept the Marquette trains from running. Roads around Sitka were completely closed by snow for days at a time, keeping the mail carrier and milk hauler from getting through.

The correspondent for the Sitka community news began listing those who were victims of the flu and other illnesses in November. By the end of the month the church and the Kempf School had been closed for several weeks, and many Grange hall meetings cancelled. Whole families were confined to their homes. This continued until early 1920 as wave after wave of the disease passed through the community and closings were used to keep the disease from spreading. A particularly bad sweep of the disease kept Dr. Black of Holton stretched to the limit making house calls.

The closing of the schools, church and cancellation of the Grange hall and Ladies Aid Society meetings, along with being a rural area, likely prevented a higher death count. The Sitka news only reported one death, that of Mrs. Peter Schmitt, who died January 12, 1918.

The Spanish flu went through in three waves covering the years 1918 and 1919. By the time it had burned itself out it is estimated that it killed between 50 and 100 million people worldwide, or approximately five percent of the world's population.

Chapter Eighteen

Tragedies

All communities have tragedies, and Sitka was no different. They had their fair share, and then some. Certain families seemed to have endured more tragic events than others.

One of the worst words one hears when living on a farm with buildings made of wood is the shout of 'Fire!' Many barns were lost over the years. Wolbrink's lost their barn, as did Mrs. William Carr. Along with the building, the contents were usually completely lost. Fred Young lost all of his hay, straw, corn fodder, bean straw, and one cow. The cause was often unknown, but in the case of J. B. Ruggles, it was lightning. Neighbors helped each other where they could. The barn of Moses Couchie was rebuilt when neighbors pitched in and hauled the needed building materials to the site. Not long after a new barn was erected.

Because so many people heated their homes with wood, the job of wood cutting was always in progress. A lot of wood had to be cut, hauled, and split to feed the flames of the furnaces. On a cold winter day in 1916 Paul Lehmann, along with Pete Schmitt, was out helping cut timber on the farm of Fred Todd near Holton. A falling tree caught the limb of another nearby tree, breaking it off. The limb fell squarely on the head of Mr. Lehmann. Though he was taken by ambulance to the hospital, where it was determined he had suffered a skull fracture, he was still able to walk on his own. But his condition later became critical and he died of his injuries. Mr. Lehmann had been a life-long resident of Sitka, having been born there in 1894. (Fremont Times Indicator, February 14, 1946)

The wood that stoked all those furnaces also lead to the prevalence of chimney fires. Mr. Bisson lost his home due to sparks from the chimney. Sometimes, as in the case of Charles Rummelt, the fire could be put out before all was lost. His roof was considerably damaged, but otherwise nothing was lost. Ernie Matthew's home was saved by use of fire extinguishers. Mrs. Beth's home and Vernon Crawford's burned to the ground with the loss of all contents. These people usually did not have insurance, so this came as a great lost to them. The experience of the Charles Kempf family was not uncommon.

> The residence of Charles Kempf and family was completely burned to the ground last Wednesday during the strong wind. It is thought sparks from the stovepipe caught in the upper portion of the house as they saw it shortly after it started and tried to put it out but were not successful the house being so dry and so strong the wind blowing. Everything was lost excepting a sewing machine, separator and a few articles of clothing. There was no insurance. The neighbors about the vicinity have been very kindly donating clothing, eatables, household utensils and money as they have a family of six small children. (Fremont Times Indicator, April 18, 1918)

Just four years later this family suffered again. On a Sunday night in October, Flora (Carmichael) Kempf, wife of Charles, went out to the barn to do her evening chores. During the course of her milking an unruly cow kicked her violently in the abdomen, causing her great harm. Flora was several months pregnant at the time. She managed to survive the night, but died early the next morning. She left behind not only her husband, but seven children, with the oldest, Oren, being only twelve years old. The baby she was carrying did not live. (Fremont Times Indicator, October 5, 1922)

Another Kempf family also had to deal with several great losses. Mrs. Lucy (Miller) Kempf had lived in the area since she was a child. She married Freeman Kempf, and together they had seven children. After a long stay at Gerber Hospital in Fremont, Lucy was taken to the University hospital in Ann Arbor. While Freeman was with his wife in Ann Arbor, the children were being taken care of back home by their grandmother. One Saturday night, close to midnight, the cries of the younger children woke the grandmother who was sleeping in an adjoining room. She found the upstairs filled with smoke and fire spreading quickly. She got everyone out safely and the Fremont rural fire department came. Thanks to the added help of neighbors, the fire was finally put out after five hours. Two milk trucks, each making four trips, brought milk cans of water to the site. The cans had been filled at nearby farmers' homes from their barn tanks.

The damage was extensive, but it would have been much worse if the children had not gained the attention of their grandmother. The second floor rooms were gutted and the roof of the house was mostly gone. Mr. Kempf was informed of the fire Sunday afternoon. His wife was listed in critical condition at the time. Three weeks later Louise (Lucy) Kempf died.

This was only part of the tragedies this family endured. Earlier they had lost a young son, Gordon, to scarlet fever after a few days illness. And, sadly, in 1940 another son, Wayne, took his own life at age 17 by hanging himself in the barn. (Fremont Times Indicator, August 28, 1941 and September 18, 1941)

Many families in Sitka came from Germany, as did John Weiler. He owned a farm on 100th St along with his wife Christina. When Chirstina died in 1909, another German family came to live with him. Mary Thill had lost her husband in Germany and was left with two young sons, John and Frank. In 1904, when the boys were about four and two years old, they emigrated to the United States. Mary Thill married her husband's brother John, who had earlier emigrated to Wisconsin. In the 1910 census they were listed as boarders of Mr. Weiler, with Mary being his housekeeper. They lived with John Weiler until his death in 1916 and then Mr. and Mrs. Thill took over the farm.

My father had many memories of the Thills. He was about the age of John Jr. and remembered when the boys started at the Jibson School. He said because they spoke mostly German they were often made fun of by the other children. John and my father, who was also of German descent, became lifelong friends. They lived on adjoining farms and spent countless hours together. So dad was there the day of the tragedy and was listed as a witness on the death certificate.

It was a Friday morning in November 1923 when John, Sr., wife Mary, and son Frank, were going about the morning milking. John smelled smoke in the upstairs of the barn and rushed to investigate. The flames exploded around him and he was quickly engulfed by the fire. He tried to escape through the upstairs barn doors, but they were barred from the outside. As the fire progressed, John's charred body was pulled from the barn where it lay next to the doors.

Though there was loss of several cattle and the barn mostly gone, the greatest loss was that of John Sr., leaving Mary a widow for the second time. The boys, though now young adults, were again without a father.

* * *

After motor vehicles began to replace travel by horse and buggy, the intersection where Dickinson and 96th St. met, Sitka corners, proved to be deadly.

George Cotham came to Sitka with his parents when he was four years old. In 1925 at age 67, a bachelor, he still lived in the same home in which he was raised, just a short distance north of the Sitka store.

On an afternoon in September George had been to the Sitka store to purchase groceries. Having done so, he placed these groceries on the east side of the road and crossed back to talk with Kenneth Proctor of Holton, the motor truck grocery man. While they were visiting, A. Crandall approached by car from the south. As he neared the corner he honked his horn in warning. Cotham quickly returned to his groceries and proceeded to kick them into the ditch, and then, for some unknown reason, he turned to go back to Mr. Proctor. He stepped squarely into the path of Mr. Crandall's auto.

Crandall and Proctor ran to Mr. Cotham's aid. He had been knocked unconscious, so they picked him up and rushed him to Gerber Hospital. He soon regained consciousness and it was determined he had several broken ribs, broken his left arm, and had multiple bruises.

A neighbor of Mr. Cotham, Douglas McDonald, visited him in the hospital. He said Mr. Cotham acknowledged he saw the car and did not hold Mr. Crandall accountable for the accident. Mr. McDonald said George had always been a very nervous man and even though he could give no reason for stepping back into the road, it was well known he was extremely afraid of automobiles.

Though the injuries did not appear to be life threatening, Mr. Cotham died five days later. A hearing was held in the office of Justice E. D. L. Evans, where upon hearing Mr. Proctor's eye witness statement, absolved Mr. Crandall of all blame. (Fremont Times Indicator, September 25, 1923)

Fast forward to 1954. Same corner. Twenty-five year old Elwin Sutton was traveling south on Dickinson towards the Sitka store on his way home. Seventeen year old Lee Homes had just left his home west of the Sitka hall and was also headed towards the Sitka store. Unknown to either driver, they were on a collision course. The impact of the two vehicles, when they met in the middle of the intersection, could be heard half a mile away.

Elwin was thrown from his car and his vehicle then rolled on top of him. Men from the store rushed to his aid and managed to get Elwin out from under his car. Sutton suffered head and internal injuries and died the next day.

No mention was made of injuries to Lee Homes, or if any tickets were issued. It appears the view of the intersection had been blocked. There was a gas pump at the store right on the corner nearest the intersection. A car had been left at the pump while the owner went inside the store. Neither driver had a good view of the other.

Elwin was the son of John and Alice Sutton. He left behind seven siblings. (Fremont Times Indicator, August 5, 1954.)

* * *

Some tragedies were premeditated.

Gilbert Kempf, son of Robert and Fannie (Miller), was born November 28, 1889 in Sitka. By the time he was 28, he had pursued many career opportunities. He had graduated from the commercial department of Ferris Institute. For three years he worked for the Escanaba Lumber Company. From there he moved on to Montana to work as a book keeper. However, after only three weeks he suffered a nervous breakdown and had to return home. He found new employment working for the Newaygo County Cow Testers Association. Due to ill health he was forced to leave this position after two years. By 1918 Gilbert was back home with his parents helping with the farming. He had taken a strong interest in raising registered dairy cows and personally owned a head of twenty Holstein.

One early morning in May, 1918 Gilbert headed to the barn with his brother to begin morning chores. Their father had already left for Fremont to take care of errands. Shortly after arriving at the barn Gilbert returned to the house and went up the steps to the upstairs bedrooms. His step-mother, Mae (Hovey) Kempf, was working in the kitchen with one of the children. Suddenly, she heard pistol fire. Fearful that the children may be in danger, she gathered them up and fled to a neighbor's home. This neighbor, along with some other men, went to the Kempf home to investigate. Carefully they climbed the stairs to find a scene that was both tragic and heartbreaking.

In one bedroom lay Lilly, Gilbert's 29 year old sister. She had been shot twice. One shot severed the juggler vein in her neck. The other bullet passed through both wrists, indicating she had put up her arms in a defensive positon. A bullet was found in her mouth.

Crossing over to the bedroom that belonged to Gilbert, they found the door locked. After gaining entry it was evident that Gilbert had taken his own life. He had fired five shots; two that went wild, two that entered his head, and one that pierced his heart. Along with the weapon the men found a lengthy letter explaining the motive for his suicide. Unusually, it was published in the Fremont paper:

> For some time I've lived not for joy in this world but to save my folks from the disgrace that was bound to come when I put death to this unbearable hell. Born with a nervous disposition I've felt this from a child up. A weakness of the nerves and mind which would be a disgrace to pass on to other children, and if 'Like begets Like' it would be sure to be that way. I can see nothing more beautiful than for the best of manhood and womanhood to pass that on to another generation but I can see nothing more disgraceful and sinful than for a weakling to pass that on to a child that has a whole life of torment and hell before it. If I thought there was a chance I'd bear it a while longer and try and get at something where this nervousness wouldn't be irritated but I don't know what that would be.
>
> I considered this while in Montana on my way home from the West when it seemed as if there could be no more enjoyment for me in this world, but when I thought of the disgrace to relatives and friends I came on home and while there was no fast improvement, I bore it. But now the time has come when I can't bear it any longer. I trust that my relatives will feel that I at least am better satisfied than before if I am successful.
>
> There must be sorrow as well as joy, but I believe there should be more joy than sorrow to make life worthwhile.
>
> As I do not envy other people, I wish you all a world of joy and happiness, at least enough to offset your sorrows. - Gilbert (Fremont Times Indicator, May 30, 1918)

No mention was made of Lilly. Some wondered if taking her life had been a last minute decision. Lilly was one year older than Gilbert, being born October 18, 1888. Twelve years previous to her death, at age 22, she had a mental breakdown from which she never recovered. Even though she had seen the best specialists of the time, she was morose, fearful, and seldom left her room. She had not spoken for several years.

Gilbert was a very popular young man with the people in Sitka and seemed to make friends easily. He was hard working and had dreams for the future in the dairy business, making this even more tragic.

* * *

Andrew (Anders) Ostberg and his wife Augusta emigrated from Sweden to the United States in 1902. With them was their six year old daughter, Lillian. They landed in Boston and lived in a variety of places, finally settling down in Egleston Township, Muskegon County where Andrew took up farming. There Lillian, now grown, met and married Elmer Walter Beth in 1915.

By 1948 the Beth's had a farm just northeast of Sitka. They had raised three children, Elman, Warren, and Carolyn, who were living on their own. Mrs. Ostberg, now 77 and widowed, lived with Lillian and Elmer.

On Saturday, March 13, Elmer Beth had gone to the market in Muskegon. Lillian Beth had decided to go skiing in the field behind their house, as there was still snow on the ground, in order to get more exercise on the advice of her doctor. This left her mother, Mrs. Ostberg, alone in the house.

As she was standing at the kitchen sink washing dishes, she heard Walter Kiesel, an 18 year old hired-hand who had worked for the Beth's for two years, enter the kitchen. When she turned around she was confronted by Walter with his arm raised as if to strike her. It was too late for Mrs. Ostberg to protect herself. He struck her four times in the head with a cultivator spring. She fell to the floor and lay in a pool of blood for the greater part of an hour, while Kiesel sat nearby waiting for her to die.

Once he was sure she was no longer alive, he picked her up and carried her upstairs, leaving a trail of blood, and dumped her on the floor of her bedroom. He returned downstairs to clean up the blood as best he could, and then waited for Mr. and Mrs. Beth to return home. It was his plan to kill them both.

It had been Walter Kiesel's job on the Beth's farm to care for the poultry. Recently he had given the baby chicks too much sulfa and several of them died. Mr. Beth had given him a tongue-lashing for this mistake. Keisel sought revenge.

Mrs. Beth, having finished her skiing, returned to the house. As she entered she was soon face to face with Kiesel, armed with a U S. Army type carbine. He pulled the trigger and nothing happened. Two more times he tried to fire the gun with no results. By then Mrs. Beth had gotten her wits about her. Sure that something had happened to her mother, she grabbed the barrel of the gun pushing it away from her just as Kiesel once more pulled the trigger. This time it fired. The bullet went through the door missing Mrs. Beth.

She started talking to him calmly. She began by saying she feared Grandma Ostberg had had some kind of accident and maybe needed help. She told Kiesel it had been her plan to have pork chops for supper, but having none she wondered if he would mind going to the Sitka store to purchase some, and while there he could call the police to tell them Mrs. Ostberg might be injured. She kept on this line of talking for some time until Kiesel finally agreed.

After he left on the tractor Mrs. Beth fled the house to nearby neighbors, Mr. and Mrs. Charles Miller. Mrs. Miller immediately called the police. At this time, though she feared the worst, Mrs. Beth still did not know what had happened to her mother.

Amazingly Kiesel did call the police when he got to the store and reported that Grandma Ostberg had been hurt and was probably dead. Officer LeCrone and Sherriff Hart hurried to the Beth residence expecting to confront a hostile Kiesel, but instead found him in a cooperative mood.

He was taken to the Fremont jail where Prosecuting Attorney J. Donald Murphy questioned him. When there arose some question about the murder weapon, Kiesel willingly returned to the Beth farm with officers and led them to the cultivator spring. He expressed no remorse.

Kiesel was examined by a panel of three psychiatrists from Grand Rapids. They found him to be 'below average intelligence, given to moody spells... erotically precocious.' In April 1918 Walter Kiesel, who had pleaded guilty to murder, was sentenced to life imprisonment at hard labor by circuit Judge Earl. Pugsley. (Fremont Times Indicator, March 16, April 15, 1948)

Chapter Ninteen

Roaring Twenties and the Great Depression

The decade after World War I was a time of enjoying life again. The 1920s were free of rationing so once more people could freely hold socials. The Ladies Aid Society and the Grange had large attendances. It was a time filled with dancing. In 1922 the Grange purchased a piano which was put to good use and in 1924 they had the largest crowd ever for a dance.

Many marriages took place after the war. Families were started. The Sitka church was thriving. Not that life was perfect—many farm auctions took place—but on the whole, the stress from the war had lifted and people were free again to enjoy life. It may not have been New York or Chicago, but it was Sitka's version of the roaring twenties.

That soon ended. In October 1929 the stock market crashed and this event was followed by a decade of hardship as the Great Depression descended on our country and on the little community of Sitka. Years of unemployment, poverty, and plunging farm incomes were a way of life for many. The purchases of durable goods, such as automobiles and washing machines, were put off as people either had no money, or thought it better to save what they had. This further pushed the economy into distress. Many farmers defaulted on loans, causing banks to fail. For the first time in the history of the United States the number of people leaving the country increased as people hoped to make a new start somewhere else.

The content of the Sitka Community News changed considerably during this decade. There were only a few Grange activities mentioned. In 1933 the Grange met to reorganize. Several members signed up and for a couple years it looked as if the Grange would survive. In 1934 they held a well-attended New Year's Eve party, and other activities followed into late 1935. But, sadly, they were unable to sustain enough interest to continue and the Sitka Grange ceased to exist. The building reverted back to the Holly Crawford family. In 1944 members of the community met to discuss the ownership of the hall, which led Alethea Crawford and other family members to deed the property to the Sitka Community Club in 1945 for one dollar.

It was difficult to keep organizations going in the thirties, but there was also a shift of interest from the Grange to the Farm Bureau. The purpose of this nonprofit organization was to make 'farming more profitable, and the community a better place to live.' Though the Farm Bureau had been in Newaygo County for years, it wasn't until 1941 that the Sitka Farm Bureau was organized.

The tough times of the 1930s also affected the Sitka Methodist Episcopal Church. In November of 1931 their pastor was reassigned. It would be many years before a regular pastor served the congregation. Services became sporadic. Now and then there would be visiting pastors, guest speakers, or performances of choirs from other churches.

One day in 1938 a man named Ben Custer, a Sunday School Superintendent from Central Baptist Church in Muskegon who was on sabbatical, happened to drive by the Sitka church with his wife, Alice, and family. It appeared the church was not being used, so he later returned to visit families in the area. He became convinced that if the doors were opened on a regular basis people would attend. And he was correct. He brought along another Sunday school teacher named Edith Burton. Together they brought in a large number of people. A church picnic at Maple Island that same year was very successful. The Ladies Aid Society even bought a new piano.

It was after many years of devotion and a new pastor was assigned, that Mr. Custer decided to take a job in northern Michigan. For many years he had owned a restaurant in Muskegon, but it was time for change. Unfortunately, the years of involvement of the Custer family in Sitka finished on a tragic note. On his way to a farewell service at Sitka with his family, Ben's car was struck by another vehicle pulling out of a gas station in Twin Lake. Ben and his family survived, but there were many months of healing. The people in the other vehicle were all killed. Many people of the area still remember Mr. Custer and fondly recall his time at Sitka church.

Chapter Twenty

Orchards Come to Sitka

After the automobile accident that killed George Cotham, his property on the northeast corner of Sitka, former ball field of the Sitka Independents, was purchased by Martin Jibson. In 1934 my father, Harold Zerlaut, secured ownership and soon the forty acres were planted with rows and rows of cherry and apple trees. This was a new development for the Sitka area as until then having an orchard meant small plantings of fruit trees near each farm house, and many at the time, including his mother, considered it a risky venture. It was the first, and largest, of four orchards that Harold Zerlaut would plant.

For the next several decades the area was filled with the activity and sounds of maintaining fruit orchards, from early spring until late fall. The grass and weeds had to be mowed and the trees were constantly sprayed for diseases and insects. The apple trees especially needed a lot of care. They were routinely pruned, and at other times the apple trees needed to be thinned of small apples so that the remaining fruit would increase in size. When there was eminent frost, father would be out with the sprayer covering the blooms with water, which then formed ice caps to protect them. I remember waking up in the wee hours of the morning listening to my father's sprayer, which could be heard a half mile away, and think how exhausted he must be.

Besides the diseases and insects there were other enemies of the orchard which needed to be managed. Deer and rabbits would dine on young fruit trees, killing several. Many remedies were tried without much success, such as tying aluminum pie pans to branches to blow in the wind, or putting Tabasco sauce on the leaves.

But the biggest enemy by far during cherry season was the arrival of crows. When one crow met up with one ripe cherry there was soon a crow free-for-all. Father obviously could not sit in the orchard all day with a shot-gun, so he did the next best thing. He set up Crow Bangers.

He used two different ones over the course of a few years. Crow Banger number one was of the crude type. It consisted of a series of large firecrackers spaced across a slow burning rope, which was then lit. As each day the firecrackers and rope needed to be replaced, it was a bit labor intensive.

Crow Banger number two was of the commercial type. It resembled a small cannon, and sounded like one, too. A slow water drip fell on a container of calcium carbide. Each time it reached a saturation point a loud explosion would occur. This happened about every twenty minutes.

This Crow Banger drip could be turned off when not needed, but since it is well-known that crows are early risers, it was turned on at the crack of dawn and turned off at dusk—for two to three weeks each July!

The explosions could be heard a mile away. Neighbors living closer got to enjoy it more, and one neighbor claimed she was about to lose her mind. At the end of cherry season the Crow Banger was packed up and put away for another year, to the relief of many.

For many years the cherries were handpicked, dumped into lugs, and then hauled on a stone boat to the truck to be taken to the cannery. Later a cherry shaker replaced handpicking. When in use, it sounded much like a machine gun. Whoever thought orchards were peaceful places, never actually lived near one.

The cherry shaker ensemble was a complex operation. Two tractors were needed. One pulled a long, narrow trough with two wheels in back and a rolled up canvas just above and along the length of the trough. A motor was connected to the power takeoff on the tractor. Four people unrolled the canvas onto the ground which had a split down the middle to allow it to surround the tree. This part of the rig was made my father to save the expense of buying a manufactured product. The other tractor, which ran the cherry shaker itself, would move a long padded arm out and secure it around a branch of cherries, then engage the shaker. The cherries would fall onto the canvas, which was then rolled up via the p.t.o on the tractor and the cherries dropped into the trough. At the bottom of the trough was a conveyor belt that moved the cherries to a large tank of very cold water where they were dumped. That tree done, the whole operation moved on to the next tree, only stopping now and then to replace a full tank with a fresh one.

The cherry juice that rained down covering the workers when the tree was shook, and the wind blowing the sand all over the sticky bodies on a hot July day, made this a nasty job. Often at the end of the day we would go straight to Mystery Lake and jump in for instant relief!

In July (for the cherries), and then again beginning in September (for the apples), many pickers would be hustling about harvesting the fruit. Enough labor for harvesting often was difficult to get, so during the 1960s and 1970s many different groups of people were brought in to help with the harvesting. The first were migrant workers who came from Mexico. It was my first experience with people who were from another country, and I was extremely curious about them, even trying out my few known Spanish words, which they usually found comical.

The migrant workers "lived" on the farm until harvest was completed, so housing had to be provided for them. Prior to the arrival of the migrants, the housing had to be inspected and approved by a government official. In those days, it did not take much to receive this official approval. For our first migrants an old chicken coop was converted into housing. It was a 20 X 36 foot building with a row of windows across the front, and a door at each end. The inside was divided into two rooms. The walls were white-washed, and the concrete floors scrubbed. A tiny sink with running water was added. A small oil furnace would furnish heat. For cooking a two-burner propane cook stove was added. Iron bedsteads were set up with tick mattresses and old Army-issue blankets. For sanitary needs, an outhouse was provided.

The migrants were extremely hard workers; their very livelihood depended upon it. From the very youngest to older adulthood, everyone worked every day. Most were unable to speak English, so one English speaking member of the group was assigned to be their spokesperson. When the crop had been completely harvested, the migrants moved to a new location—sometimes to a farm nearby; other times to a different state—to pick crops that were in season at the time.

Sometimes the migrants were housed on the farm of my brother Allen, who lived next door. His wife Margie had quite a shock one morning when she opened her backdoor and stepped out. There, in a tub of water filled by a nearby hose, sat a naked man taking a bath!

Some of the migrants were used to help grade apples rather than pick them. This was also one of my jobs each day after I got home from school. At that time the companies buying the apples insisted on them being within a certain size limit, and of course, without blemish. For this job my father purchased a commercial set up. It was a long, narrow table with railings along the sides to keep the apples from rolling off. Along the table were rollers that were constantly turning. The table reached the width of the barn upstairs. At one end a person would continually dump crates of apples onto the rollers. People would be placed on both sides of the table. As the apples rolled by we pulled out any apples that did not fit the requirements of the apple company. These apples were put into crates, and later were sold as "seconds". The qualifying apples continued down to the end, where they were again placed in crates and loaded on to the truck for delivery.

Once a group of non-Hispanic people came from the southern part of the United States to pick apples. There were about twenty-five people—three families in all—aunts, uncles and cousins of all ages, from young children to adults. They arrived in a large, white, flatbed truck with rails on the sides, and a canvas covering across the top. This is where most of them traveled. Due to the number of people, the converted chicken coop alone was not large enough to house them. Father enclosed his utility

Chapter Twenty: Orchards Come to Sitka

shed where he kept his tractors where many of them slept.

They were such good workers that father had difficulty keeping up with them. Even though my dad did not normally work on Sundays, these people insisted on working every single day. It wasn't long before the crop was harvested. He was so impressed by them that he tried to hire them the following year, but they were not available.

One group came that did not live on site. These were nonviolent prisoners from the Muskegon County jail who were let out on day-furloughs to work. There was a man in charge whose job it was to make sure they worked and to get them back to the jail on time. If one of the workers did not work hard enough, he was not allowed to come back, as dad had to sign papers saying they had done their job.

The man in charge of the prisoners routinely left about noon, saying he was going somewhere to pick up lunch and would be back soon. My father had been concerned about apples disappearing, but could not quite figure out who was taking them. One day as the man was getting into his car to leave for lunch, my father noticed how low the car was sitting to the ground. When the trunk was opened it was full of apples the man was taking to sell. Father decided the trunk had been filled every day at noon, then again at the end of the picking day. Needless to say, this was the end of the prisoner help. The man who was supposed to watch them was the one who actually needed watching.

But this was not the first time prisoners were used to help with the harvest. My father, not known for being chatty, could not resist each cherry season telling the story about the German Prisoners of War who helped pick cherries during World War II. Yes, German POWs were right there on the corner of Sitka. Just how these POWs ended up in Sitka will be explained in another chapter.

Chapter Twenty-one

War Again

Life is all about change, and change was once again on the horizon. In September 1939 Nazi Germany invaded Poland, beginning World War II. The United States had resisted officially entering the war for nearly two years. The bombing of Pearl Harbor by the Japanese, December 7, 1941, changed all that. The United States declared war against Japan, and in response, on December 11, 1941, under an agreement Japan had made with Hitler, Germany declared war on the United States.

The United States had been gearing up for war for some time. In 1940 a new federal statute called for the registration and fingerprinting of all resident aliens, which constituted about 220 people in Newaygo County. Failure to register, refusal to be fingerprinted, or making false statements, would be met with $1000 in fines and six months' imprisonment. However, this statement was issued which put the situation into a better context:

> Although the primary object of the alien registration law is to uncover 'fifth columnists', government officials stress the fact that just because an individual is an alien, he should not be suspected of being connected with subversive activities.
>
> The registration does not carry with it any stigma or implication of hostility toward those who while they may not be citizens, are loyal to this country and its institutions. Most of the aliens in this country are people who came here because they believed and had faith in the principles of American democracy, and they are entitled to and must receive full protection of the law. (Fremont Times Indicator, August 29, 1940)

That same year 1,915 men between the ages of 21 and 35 were drafted in Newaygo County.

Chapter Twenty-one: War Again

In anticipation of war, the county began one of several drives that lasted throughout the war. The first was an aluminum drive which brought in 1089 pounds of metal. The aluminum was sent to smelters to supply defense contracts. The money was to be used for purchase of trainer planes for the Army and Navy. (The Air Force, not yet organized, was not a separate military service until 1947.)

In another drive for scrap iron a $25 defense bond was awarded to the person bringing in the most scrap. The county Salvage for Victory committee reminded people for every three pounds of steel manufactured, one pound of scrap iron was needed.

When a metal drive went lagging, a reprimand would appear in the newspaper like the following one by J. M. Hopwood, President, War Materials Inc.: 'If we don't get busy, there will be plenty of scrap. The enemy will provide it, with bombings, and we will be picking pieces of scrap off the streets and out of the bodies of American citizens. We've got to wake up.' (Fremont Times Indicator, October 3, 1942) This certainly got right to the point, and these half-page rebukes succeeded in achieving the goals. It was later noted that 420 lbs. of scrap metal could make 210 semi-automatic carbines, 850 lbs. could be converted into 100 armor piercing projectiles, and if you donated one tractor you could be responsible for providing 580 machine guns. If five tractors were given they could be made into one tank.

Housewives were urged to purchase fresh foods in order to save metal used for cans for the war effort. If an appliance or water heater needed to be repaired, the old part first had to be turned in before a new part would be issued. Any metals that could be salvaged were considered critical to the needs of war. It was expected that all Americans would do their part to make metal available.

There were also drives for service organizations. For those who served in World War I, the American Red Cross was instrumental in their well-being. This was true of this war as well. There were fund drives to provide money or materials for the Red Cross. The Red Cross in Newaygo County received 700 yards of material and a call went out for volunteers to sew clothing for the war effort. Later these same volunteers were asked to make 39,000 surgical dressings.

The United Service Organizations, known as the USO, provided morale building activities for the servicemen. They used entertainers and comedians to keep our armed forces connected to home and family. A county drive to raise $3,590 as their part of a national drive for thirty-two million dollars was held in 1942. There was a vital need 'to provide recreation and a home-like atmosphere for men who were suddenly taken from their regular routine of life and placed in large camps to learn ways of war.' (Fremont Times Indicator, May 21, 1942)

The most aggressive drive, though, was the drive to sell War Savings Bonds. Beginning in 1942 the push for the sale of War Bonds was relentless. Americans were expected to invest at least ten percent of their income in War Bonds every pay day to support the forces fighting the war. Many articles were published showing how this money was being spent. For instance, it was explained that semi-automatic weapons were being manufactured at the rate of one per minute at a cost of $85 each. And further:

> The army's fighter planes are the finest in the world and develop speeds up to 400 miles an hour. They cost approximately $160,000 each, provide fighter escorts for huge flying fortresses, and combine speeds, range and altitude and blistering fire power.
>
> War Saving Bonds will help pay for them and the American people are committed to at least ten percent of their income to finance their cost in War Bonds. Every American buying his share every pay day will make it comparatively easy to supply our army and navy and air corps with these supreme Eagles of the air. (Fremont Times Indicator, July, 23, 1942)

War Bonds also provided millions of first aid kits for emergency treatment. They were carried by servicemen and were needed by the Red Cross in field hospitals.

The list of materials needed and their cost continued throughout the war, leaving no doubt what was expected from the American citizens. And it was as easy as going to your local Kroger store to purchase a War Bond.

The various drives were some of the less stressful ways of helping the war effort. Those who had gone through rationing in WWI were familiar with its difficulties, but there were even more shortages this time around. In May 1942 applications for sugar ration books reached 18,829 in Newaygo County. Each stamp was good for two weeks and allowed one pound of sugar per person. During canning season housewives were allowed one pound of sugar for every four quarts of finished canned fruit.

A housewife in need of a pressure cooker for canning faced a shortage due to the lack of available metal. Newaygo County was allotted 58 pressure cookers in the summer of 1943. Those hoping to get a pressure cooker had to fill out an application and had to have processed at least 300 quarts of vegetables or meat the previous year. This scarcity affected rural women, like those in Sitka, in particular, as they raised most of their own food. Groups of women were encouraged to share one pressure cooker, which would be inconvenient to say the least, during a busy canning season.

Coffee was also in short supply as shipping became limited. Most ships were being used in the war effort, and the Germans scouted shipping lanes for merchant ships. The military were given priority, leaving coffee rations back home to one pound per person every six weeks. People were encouraged to stretch coffee by drinking it very weak or adding chicory. It was not a popular ration and was the first to be restored after war's end.

In October 1942, just in time for the winter heating season, fuel oil began to be rationed. Adding to the heating problem, coal delivery was limited. A consumer had to purchase one ton of coal or more before a delivery would be made. The slogan used at the time was 'Order no less than a ton until the war is won.' There was sound reasoning behind this, as the nation, and its dependence on oil, had changed dramatically since the last war.

During the previous war many people were still traveling by horse and wagon. The loss of any animal was often reported in the Sitka News, as it affected the livelihood of one of their neighbors. When it came to horses, however, the reporting reached a whole new level. There were even horse obituaries! The following are just two local examples.

> While on the road to Fremont last Friday the horse known as Spike, owned by John Wilson, dropped dead. Spike was imported from France, from there he came to Chicago and for many years has been owned by people around here. (Fremont Times Indicator, December 25, 1912)

> Old Doc, a horse belonging to Henry Zerlaut, died last week at the age of 25 years, Mr. Zerlaut having owned him since he (the horse) was five years old. (Fremont Times Indicator, May, 30, 1917)

As horse travel diminished the need for gasoline for automobiles and rubber tires became much more in demand. So automobiles and everything associated with them became as important to rural life as horses had been. When World War II began there were massive shortages of these commodities. This led to the rationing of gasoline and rubber products.

In order to receive a gas ration book a certificate of ownership for the vehicle had to be presented. The owner was allowed five tires, four on the car plus one spare. The serial numbers of those tires had to be included on the form. The gas cards allowed the owner four gallons of gasoline a week. This would certainly impede the movement of people, and for those in rural areas, just going to town for supplies would eat up gasoline allotments fairly fast. Many activities were cancelled. The social get-togethers that people needed were cut to a minimum.

Even though there were different classifications of gas cards giving merchants eight gallons a week, it was thought by the coal company that it was prudent to keep deliveries limited to one ton to save on gasoline

Chapter Twenty-one: War Again

and tires.

The shortage of rubber not only affected tires, but anything else that had rubber as part of its materials. By 1942 certificates were needed to obtain rubber work boots and shoes with rubber soles. People applying needed to establish proof of need and surrender their unusable footwear.

Finally, there were two other drives that took place. The U. S Victory Paper Campaign called for the recycling of magazines, newspapers, corrugated paper, and cardboard boxes.

> The shortage of pulpwood and the millions of tons of food, ammunition and equipment sent overseas weekly to the American and Allied forces has created an urgent need for paper which cannot be met adequately unless all of the waste paper obtainable is turned in for reprocessing... Reprocessed waste paper is used in the manufacture of air force emergency packs, signal flares, fuses, gas mask and grenade containers and incendiary bombs. (Fremont Times Indicator, January 1, 1944)

The most unusual drive was the salvaging of fats. The different applications to which fats could be put to use were quite remarkable. First of all, the fat had to be collected. Housewives were urged to cut off fat from meat and take it to a participating butcher where they would be paid a few cents a pound. The dealer would then pass the fat on to rendering firms.

> 'More fats are needed by the war industries which are producing high explosives, and the women of this community can aid in helping to supply this necessary ingredient of glycerin by saving all of the waste kitchen fats which have previously been discarded... Saving just a tablespoonful of waste fat at a time may seem rather insignificant but only 31 tablespoonfuls are needed to make a pound, and a pound of salvaged fat provides enough glycerin to fire four anti-aircraft shells or to manufacture a half-pound of dynamite.' (Fremont Times Indicator, March 25, 1943)

And again, we read in 1945 that:

> Newaygo County's 5,075 families can fill an entire day's medicinal

needs of 1,903 battlefront casualties if each home will save one tablespoon of waste kitchen fat, it was estimated today by the nation's largest single collector of this vital war material.

'The value of the 1,928,000 pounds salvaged by our customers throughout the nation last year is evident in the fact that a single pound of fat will process about 260 quarts of life-giving blood plasma. The increasing tempo of the war has intensified the need for drugs, ointments and acids to ease pain and lessen mortality among our soldiers as well as for synthetic rubber, protective coatings and other vital war materials...even a tablespoon, or half ounce, of used fat will help make enough small pox vaccine for 75 injections.

Other vital medication for which household fats are required includes tannic acid used in treatment of burns, some insulating for shock victims, tinctures of opium and gentian to ease pain, sulfadiazine ointments for treating abrasions and fungus growths and nitro-glycerin tablets as a heart stimulant. (Fremont Times Indicator, March 8 1945)

All of this collecting and rationing would have had a major impact on the lives of Sitka residents. I know that I will never look at fat in the same way ever again!

In August 1942 Newaygo County participated in its first blackout test. This test was done to train local civil defense organizations. Lights in all participating counties were to be turned off at 11 p.m. for 30 minutes. A few months later the public warning system, using new Air Raid Signals, was tested.

At 9:30 when the red flash signal came announcing the complete blackout, the traffic halted completely. Some confusion resulted in one section of the city (Fremont) during this period when a few residents mistook the three minute signal for the 'All Clear' signal and turned on their lights but alert Sector Wardens remedied the situation.

At 9:43 the second blue flash period started and traffic resumed with low beam headlights. The white 'All-Clear' signal came at 9:55 p.m., indicating that the 'raiders' had gone and the blackout had ended. (Fremont Times Indicator, June 17, 1943)

County listening posts had also been set up. The airplane detector stations were delayed due to the lack of wire, but the Fremont Chamber of Commerce donated wire used for holiday street lighting so the project could be completed. There were five regular stations, plus several secondary listening posts in the homes around the county. Volunteers worked two hour shifts.

The wire shortage also affected the telephone service. Copper, aluminum, steel, and other materials needed to expand telephone lines were more urgently needed for planes, tanks, ships and guns to win the war. Constant newspaper and radio reminders were used to keep people off the phones unless absolutely necessary to keep lines open for war business.

> Telephone lines today are crowded as never before. And Long Distance lines between all Michigan points and war production centers are carrying some of the heaviest traffic in the country.
>
> War calls must go through promptly. In normal times we'd enlarge the telephone system to handle the increased load. We can't today, because the materials required for sufficient telephone expansion are even more urgently needed on the fighting fronts. (Fremont Times Indicator, July 30, 1942)

One ad admonished people by telling them, 'whatever you do, do NOT call your Aunt Agnes on Christmas!'

Many of these drives, rationings, blackouts, and tests were going on simultaneously. The war was continuously front and center in people's daily lives. Today we still have many who are serving our country and are constantly in harm's way, but unless that service person is someone we know and care about, we are so removed from the daily efforts of war that we are only reminded of it when we watch the news. It does not affect our daily lives and comfort as it did for those who lived in Sitka during WWII and the millions of others in our country at that time. They were face to face with the effects of war from the minute they set foot out of bed. Hard to imagine today having our phone usage cut and our shoes rationed.

So how did the people of Sitka respond? Just as you might expect they would. They scrimped and saved and continued on as best they could. Many helped the war effort through the Farm Bureau.

> Members were asked to bring their donation of a bushel of wheat or its equivalent to the January meeting. The wheat will be turned over to the Junior Farm Bureau to aid them in obtaining the Newaygo County quota towards the purchase of a $10,000 War Bond. Chrystal Kempf reported that all the boxes of Christmas goodies had been mailed to the boys in the service. (Fremont Times Indicator, December 17, 1942)

> The Sitka Farm Bureau members enjoyed a hard times and Halloween party at the Sitka hall Friday evening. The party was sponsored by the organization to raise funds for Christmas gifts to be sent to member men and women in the service. A total of $21.70 was raised. (Fremont Times Indicator, October 28, 1943)

This fund raiser was held again the following year in October to raise money for Christmas boxes.

Just as was the case with the Grange, Farm Bureau members often joined together to discuss topics of importance, both locally and nationally, to the community. After a business meeting in February 1943, the members gathered around a radio to listen to a speech given by President Roosevelt.

In an address at a membership meeting, a representative from the Ludington Farm Bureau stated,

> In the crises which our country faces, Democracy is threatened from within and without. Farmers must organize if they are to help save Democracy. A fair share of the national income for agriculture is necessary to the prosperity of America. An organization speaks more loudly than an individual and we can accomplish a great deal more both for agriculture and for our country if we work together. (Fremont Times Indicator, January 2, 1942)

At another meeting that year the topic of the month was, 'Equality of Sacrifice in this War'. This centered on trade and tariff conditions.

Chapter Twenty-two

The Labor Shortage

As the war progressed, the number of farm auction sales accelerated. Many sales took place in 1941, but the number doubled in 1942. The induction of so many men into the service left farmers short-handed when it came to workers. Those who were available for work found higher paying jobs in the booming factories. By 1943 the farm labor shortage was critical. There just were not enough men to plant or harvest crops. Meeting future demands was going to be difficult.

But it was not only the farms that were affected. Many women were being hired to replace men who had left for war. And yet, places such as Gerber Products Company, still had a lack of help necessary to continue to run the plant.

In 1944 there were 75,000 German prisoners of war in the United States. Since there was such a labor shortage, it was suggested the prisoners fill the labor gap. The prisoners, it was argued, had to be housed and fed whether they worked or not. However, it was also stressed they should only be used where local help was inadequate so as not to take jobs away from American citizens.

Certain steps had to be taken before this could be set into place. First, the people of the community had to agree to have a prisoner of war camp in their midst. Secondly, the War Manpower Commission had to certify there was indeed a shortage of labor. The Army had to give its approval as it would furnish housing and food for both prisoners and guards.

Gerber Products stated they could use about 150 prisoners. They received the endorsement of the Chamber of Commerce and both local unions. It was understood that these prisoners would be moved out of the area when they were no longer needed so they would not be in competition with local labor.

Chapter Twenty-two: The Labor Shortage

By June, 274 prisoners had arrived from Fort Custer. They arrived in a long caravan consisting of forty-one army trucks. Of these, twenty-three carried prisoners and seventeen were filled with supplies and equipment. That must have been a very impressive convoy as it moved through the little town of Fremont. (Fremont Times Indicator, March 16 and June 1, 1944)

The encampment was established at the rear of the Gerber plant. On August 3, 1944 the Fremont Times Indicator published an exclusive report on camp life after an authorized visit.

> Row after row of neatly aligned tents first meet the eye as one approaches the German War Prisoner camp, east of the Gerber Products Company plant, where the past two months prisoners have contributed more than 88,000 man hours of work on farms in this community and at the plant. Almost simultaneous, however you see the army guards at their elevated posts alert for an emergency...The prison enclosure is separated from the soldiers' quarters by a high, many stranded barbed wire fence. Armed guards are stationed in elevated look-out posts. The prisoners' tents are arranged in rows with wide spaces between them for better observation.
>
> The treatment accorded them [the prisoners] is standardized by international law under the Geneva Agreement. Only those who volunteer are accepted for work. The government (U. S. Treasury) is paid the regular rate of pay in this area and the prisoners receive 80 cents a day in script from the Army. Under Army regulations and international law they may be used only for work not directly related to the war effort under the same working conditions as free labor...The men work eight hours a day and cannot be away from camp more than 12 hours in any one day, including travel time. A maximum 48 hour week of six days is also provided by law.
>
> More than $100 of athletic equipment has been assigned to the camp from Fort Custer for the prisoner's use. Soccer is their favorite game and recently they began leveling a field adjoining the enclosure. Moving pictures are also shown.
>
> Many of the men have German Bibles which they read. They are free to worship as they please. Services in the German language are held each Sunday.

A German English dictionary used in the English class is the best seller in the camp and many of the prisoners save their script until they have enough to buy one.

The men have their own post exchange where they can buy cigarettes, razor blades, a few articles of clothing, candy, soft drinks and incidentals...The prisoners receive considerable mail from Germany and are allowed to write one letter and one post card each week under the regulations. Medical services are also available... In front of their tents the prisoners have planted many flowers and plants which have been given them by Fremont residents....

But even with these seemingly good conditions, there were three men who decided it was their duty to escape. One night the men, who were all in their twenties and unable to speak English, cut wire and crawled under on their stomachs into a nearby cornfield.

Once their escape was discovered, the FBI, state, county, local, and military police began a search for the missing men. Their descriptions were broadcast on local radio stations. Two army-trained dogs were summoned to aid in the search of a swamp after a woman believed she had seen one of the men. Several other 'sightings' also proved false. As one might imagine, the residents of Sitka would have been quite alarmed at this development, wondering whether these enemy soldiers could be in their area.

The three escaped German prisoners were finally discovered a few days later in an unused barn two miles north of Hart by a hired farm hand, Francis Clay, when he heard water running in an unused section of a barn. He ordered the men out and they complied without resistance. Tired and hungry, they appeared more than happy to surrender and were returned to the prison camp. It seems they had thought they would reach the sea coast by foot in about 30 days, and from there find their way home. Captain Stricklund stated that: 'The men are receiving the same disciplinary action for their escape that an army man who has gone A. W. O. L. would receive. (Fremont Times Indicator, July 13 and July 20, 1944)

Chapter Twenty-two: The Labor Shortage

There was much scrutiny by citizens about the treatment of these prisoners. Some felt they were being coddled. Others worried about the safety of citizens working in the plant with these men. It was explained that the International Red Cross was duty bound to report any condition that violated the Geneva Convention regarding treatment of prisoners.

> As for danger to citizens working in the factory, they were mostly segregated from the prisoners. Only supervisory personnel had contact with them and then only when it was absolutely necessary. (Fremont Times Indicator, February 8, 1945)

It was a little different for the farmers who used the prisoners to breach the labor shortage. When my father arrived for the first time at the prisoner camp with his flatbed truck with rails on the side, he was loaded up with prisoners, and an armed guard was appointed to go with them to the cherry orchard. When the guard climbed into the cab beside my father, he questioned why he was in the truck instead of on the back with the prisoners. He was told not to worry, as the prisoners weren't going anywhere.

My father paid the Army the going wage for work done. The prisoners in turn were given 80 cents a day for their work in script which could be used at the prisoner commissary.

When the work for the day was done, they were loaded back on to the truck and returned to camp. Sometimes, when the weather was very hot, my father and the guard took the men to Mystery Lake for a swim before returning them to camp. But this practice came to an end when, one day on the way back to the camp, with dad tooling along and the guard probably involved in idle chit-chat with him, one of the prisoners either fell off the back of the truck or was pushed. That he was missing was not noticed until they arrived at the camp. About two hours later he arrived, panting and shouting that he was not trying to escape!

As far as can be established, my father was the only Sitka resident to make use of German POWs. He felt he was doing them a favor as the men were quite eager to get out of camp and into the countryside. It also would have provided quite a talking point around Sitka with the truckload of German soldiers regularly showing up to help pick cherries.

As the war drew to a close in October 1945, prisoners began to be transferred out and the camp disbanded. At the peak of the prisoner of war use there were 402 German prisoners at the Gerber site. There was another prisoner camp located near Grant. This was a temporary tent-camp that provided workers for agricultural use only. It also closed in October, bringing to a close the story of POW work camps in Newago County—and German soldiers picking cherries in Sitka!

Chapter Twenty-three

Those Who Served—World War II

Through all the rationing and drives, the biggest sacrifices by far were by the men and women who served and the families left waiting for their safe return. This included many people who had ties to Sitka—so many in fact, that there is not space enough to detail all their courage and service. The small representation that follows is to honor all the men and women who put their lives on the line, and in one case, lost it.

More than ever before, women were becoming involved in the war effort. Positions in factories were filled by women to cover the labor shortage. Others sought to be part of the 150,000 women who served in the Women's Army Corps (WAC), which was created in 1942.

The idea of women in uniform, other than Army nurses, was not readily accepted by the Army or by people in general, but the shortage of manpower for necessary jobs compelled them to use women as a new resource. Most of the WACs served stateside, but others were found in Europe, North Africa, New Guinea, and the aftermath of the invasion of Normandy.

They filled positons as switchboard operators, postal clerks, drivers, stenographers, and clerk-typists. They also maintained and repaired small arms and heavy weapons, even though they were not allowed to use them.

Other women decided to put their effort into the Army Nurse Corps. These 59,000 women found themselves close to front lines, in hospitals, and on train and plane transports. Due to these highly skilled women, many fewer men died from their injuries.

There were shortages of specialized nurses of anesthesia which the Army sought to remedy by special training. One Sitka woman, though, was already prepared. Alethea Crawford, granddaughter of Holly and Luella Crawford, was born in Sitka on September 12, 1911, to George and Alta Crawford. After graduating from Fremont High School, she attended Bronson School of Nursing. She followed this with more study at the University of Minnesota where she received a degree from The School of Anesthesia. When the war broke out she joined the Army Nurse Corps and was assigned to serve at Starks General Hospital in Charleston, South Carolina. Later she became part of the staff at West Point Military Academy in New York. Following the end of the war Alethea became superintendent of Gerber Memorial Hospital.

In 1942 another Sitka woman also entered the Army Nurse Corps. Barbara MacDonald was the daughter of Douglas and Elsie (Kempf) MacDonald. As a 1936 graduate of Fremont High School, she went on to complete nurses training at the Hackley School of Nursing. She was given a leave of absence and sent to Scott Field in Illinois.

As with many families, Barbara also had a sibling in the service. Her brother, Ward MacDonald, was commissioned as a Second Lieutenant in the field artillery of the U. S. Army. He was awarded the Soldier's Congressional Medal for heroism at sea on October 26, 1942 at the time of the sinking of the transport ship, the President Coolidge.

> After seeing that his own men were evacuated, Lieut. MacDonald went to the foyer of 'C' Deck forward and assisted in the evacuation of men through that area. He stayed until all the men had cleared the deck and then upon orders of his commander went up the rope and out the gangway.
>
> Through an opening in the starboard side of the ship, then laying on its port side, he assisted two officers in the rescue of another by means of a rope through the opening. The last officer remaining could not be brought up before the ship went completely under.'
> (Fremont Times Indicator, March 18, 1943)

Lt. MacDonald was promoted to Captain in November 1944. His parents only knew that he was 'somewhere' in New Guinea. He also participated in campaigns in Guadalcanal and New Georgia.

The following year he was awarded the Bronze Star Medal for his heroism in the Philippine Islands. The citation read,

> For heroic achievement in connection with military operations against the enemy in the vicinity of New Bosoboso, Rizal Province, Luzon Philippine Islands on 20 April 1945. Captain MacDonald, in command of an artillery liaison section, conducted accurate and effective close-in artillery fires on an enemy counter-attack. During the performance of this heroic achievement, Captain MacDonald was subjected to enemy fire, and it was only through sheer intestinal fortitude that he accomplished the mission. Captain MacDonald's great personal courage, coolness under fire, and devotion to duty were an inspiration to the members of his command. (Fremont Times Indicator, June 12, 1945)

Upon the conclusion of the war, another medal was bestowed. Captain MacDonald was awarded the Silver Star Medal for gallantry in action against the enemy at Ipo Dam on May 17, 1945. In a letter to his parents, Leonard F. Wing Major General stated, 'The war has ended and the admiration that I have for courage and devotion to duty of men with whom I serve, like your son, is only equaled by that of a grateful nation, in token of which this honor has been presented.' (Fremont Times Indicator, October 11, 1945)

Another pair of siblings, sons of Elmer and Lillian (Ostberg) Beth, joined the U. S. Army Air Corps, and later the Air Force, making this their life-long career. Elman, the older of the two, majored in engineering and business administration at the University of Michigan. In 1939 he volunteered for service as an Aviation Cadet and later became an Advanced Flying Instructor.

> [In 1944 Captain Beth was] 'appointed a Squadron Commander of the 15th Air Force B-24 Liberator unit in Italy. His Squadron has played an outstanding role in the bombing offensive against Nazi industrial and communications targets in the Balkans, Northern Italy and Southern Germany. He had previously served as Operations Officer of another Squadron in his group.

Captain Beth, who is a First Pilot, has taken part in numerous missions over German-occupied territory. As a result of his successful work, he has received his Air Medal for 'meritorious achievement while participating in sustained operational activities against the enemy. (Fremont Times Indicator, June 29, 1944)

Captain Elmer Beth went on to serve in the United States Air Force until 1965.

Warren Andrews Beth also graduated from Fremont High School, and then attended the University of Michigan for three years. He enlisted as an Army Aviation Cadet in 1940, following in the footsteps of his brother Elman.

In October 1942 he led the flight of army bombers which caused the sinking of two Japanese destroyers off Kiska, Alaska.

The attack was made in the face of heavy enemy anti-aircraft fire and the encounter lasted 45 minutes. Five bombs are reported to have struck the first destroyer and four hits were scored on the second Jap craft. The American flyers saw the crew of the first destroyer go overboard after a series of explosions. Many of the Japanese sailors could be seen among the wreckage by the American flyers. Smoke from the two destroyers was evidence of the destructive force of the attack. (Fremont Times Indicator, October 22, 1942)

For his skill and heroism in leading the formation of B-26 bombers in this battle, Captain Beth was awarded the Distinguished Flying Cross.

Shortly after this attack Captain Beth was promoted to major, and at a speech he gave to the Fremont Chamber of Commerce when he was home on leave, he had this to say about the Japanese pilots and the area of the Aleutian Islands where he was stationed.

Japanese pilots are well trained and like to drop down from high altitudes on lone ships whenever the opportunity arises. The Zero, however, while a fast altitude gainer, does not provide much protection for the pilot. The plane has no armor plate nor does it provide protection for the gasoline supply.

Many of the air fields taken in the Aleutian chain of islands from the Japs were poorly laid out and constructed and showed little regard for engineering principles.' (Fremont Times Indicator, September 9, 1943)

In all, Warren Beth, who was later promoted to colonel, flew 41 combat missions against Germany with two forced parachute landings. He was awarded the Purple Heart, Distinguished Flying Cross, and Air Medal with three Oak Leaf Clusters, making him one of the most decorated aviators of the Second World War.

After the war Warren continued his career as a military pilot. In 1963 he was stationed at Cape Canaveral and was in charge of a 50-plane Operation Group. It was his job to direct his 1000 men in the aerial tracking and recovery of astronaut Leroy Gordon 'Gordo' Cooper, Jr. in the 22-orbit flight of Mercury 9 (Fremont Times Indictor, May 13, 1963). Colonel Beth's mother, Lillian Beth, whose own courage and wits under great duress had saved her life when she had encountered her mother's murderer in her home in 1948, was there to watch the successful shot into orbit.

* * *

A common sight in Sitka and many other towns during the war was a white banner with navy blue stars hanging in the windows of homes—one star for each family member serving. Three sisters, daughters of Gustaveous (Gustav) and Anna Kempf, all born in the 1890s in Sitka, had the shared worry of having one or more of their children in the war at the same time. Barbara MacDonald and her brother Ward were the children of Elsie (Kempf) and Douglas MacDonald.

Elsie's older sister, Katherine, along with husband Herman Zerlaut, also had two stars of their own on a banner. The oldest son, Elwin 'Lavern' Zerlaut, attended Ferris State College. He joined the Army Air Corps in 1942. Lavern flew numerous missions as a gunner on a B-17 over Germany. He was awarded the European-African-Middle Eastern Ribbon and promoted to Second Lieutenant in 1944.

After the war, Lavern married Jacquelyn Frost. She held the unusual distinction of having had her own civilian pilot's license before the war. When war broke out she joined the WASPs. During the war she was stationed at Avenger Field in Sweetwater, Texas. She ferried training planes to schools and fighter planes to their points of departure as a solo pilot.

Younger brother Herman Walter Zerlaut attended Marquette University, graduating with a degree in Mechanical Engineering. Later, he received a degree in Architectural Design from the Art Institute of Chicago.

Walter served in the Navy, doing duty in the Pacific Theater. In the last part of the war he participated in transporting the wounded to U. S. hospitals.

The third sister, Christina 'Tina' Kempf, former Kempf School teacher, married Alpheus Parisian. Their son, Stanford, was born in 1923. They saw their only son go off to war at just 19 years of age.

Stanford was in the Infantry Division, and in December 1944 he was deep into Luxembourg when the last German offensive campaign began, which came to be known as The Battle of the Bulge.

> The U. S Army Center of Military History states that in 'late 1944, during the wake of the Allied forces' successful D-Day invasion of Normandy, France, it seemed as if the Second World War was all but over. On Dec. 16, with the onset of winter, the German army launched a counteroffensive that was intended to cut through the Allied forces in a manner that would turn the tide of war in Hitler's favor. ... Early on the misty winter morning of Dec. 16, 1944, more than 200,000 German troops and nearly 1000 tanks launched Adolf Hitler's last bid to reverse the ebb in his fortunes ...

Within days, Patton's Third Army had relieved Bastogne, and to the north, the 2nd U. S. Armored Division stopped enemy tanks short of the Meuse River on Christmas. Through

January, American troops, often wading through deep snow drifts, attacked the sides of the shrinking bulge until they had restored the front and set the stage for the final drive to victory.

But it came at an enormous cost. The largest and bloodiest battle of World War II ended on January 25, 1945. Estimated losses vary depending on the source, but it appears that from the Department of Defense and the United States Department of the Army that there were 80,000-100,000 American casualties. This included the wounded, missing, and the dead. An approximate number of dead is given as 19,000.

Technical Sergeant Stanford Parisian was one of the fatally wounded. He would never be seen by his family again. He died on December 27, 1944 at the age of 21. He was awarded posthumously the Silver Star Medal, The Bronze Star Medal, and the Purple Heart. He was buried in the Luxembourg American Cemetery, which contains the remains of 5,076 American service members.

Chapter Twenty-four

The Post-War Years

Being born in 1946, I was part of a generation called the "baby-boomers". Over the years I watched as Sitka began to diminish in its overall footprint. I have never regretted spending my grade school years at Jibson School, and have always felt I gained a wonderful beginning education there. Children who were just a little younger did not get to experience the joys of a one-room school. In 1951 there were still sixty-one rural schools in Newaygo County; by the 1960s most of them had closed. The Kempf School annexed to the Fremont School system in 1962. The Jibson School followed suit in 1966.

The Kempf School property was sold to Harvey Matthews, and the building eventually torn down. Allen Zerlaut bought the Jibson property and turned it into a home which he rented out. In 1976 fire destroyed the home and all the possessions of the Roman Halasinski family. With the help of nearby neighbors, the family of eight escaped through windows and no one was seriously hurt. The property is now the home of Steve and Robin Zerlaut.

Even as the local schools began to close, the community still cared deeply about the learning of their young people. Many of us were soon involved in the 4-H organization. This program was designed for young people to give them hands-on learning skills outside the realm of the school classroom. Local adult volunteers shared their knowledge in classes, which followed a spring-summer and fall-winter schedule. I can still recite the 4-H pledge which began each general meeting:

Chapter Twenty-four: The Post-War Years

"I pledge...
my head to clearer thinking,
my heart to greater loyalty,
my hands to larger service,
and my health to better living,
  for my club,
    for my community,
      my country,
        and my world."

This pledge was represented by a 4-H clover pin which we wore, having an "H" on each leaf.

The classes focused on basic farm and homemaking skills, developed over time. Each year you participated you were given more difficult tasks to complete. At the end of each period the students were given the chance to show their accomplishments, either at the 4-H Fair held in Fremont during the month of August, or the Style Show held at the Fremont Community Building in the spring, where we were able to model our sewing projects.

When I was ten, I was anxious about moving from beginning sewing, which involved making an apron and hemming dishtowels, to sewing a dress, with Rose Smith as my leader. My project was a beautiful little red sailor dress with middy collar and navy blue braid. Alas, the night before the style show, I came down with chicken pox. Being spring, my mother put the dress away to save for school in the fall. Imagine my dismay, when in the fall it no longer fit! I never did get to wear my dress, but my younger cousin wore it often.

Baking and cooking classes were taught as well. Marjorie Smith remembers walking with Sandy and Julie Kempf to cooking classes taught by Margaret Jibson. On the way home they would stop at the store for ice cream. With 4-H cookbook in hand, I made a variety of dishes and baked goods for my family. However, since brownies were the item to be taken to the fair to be judged, I made batch after batch of brownies to hone my skills. Though we all loved brownies, by the end of summer we were pretty grateful the fair season was over.

Both boys and girls participated in raising and showing a variety of animals. My brother Bob, under the direction of leader Max Kempf, took young dairy calves to the fair. Another time he took his horse, Colonel.

My sister Arlene raised a young steer for the fair. It was known in advance that at the end of the fair the steer would be part of the stock auction. Though she took her earnings from the sale of her prize steer to buy a sewing machine, she was never to do it again. She was so attached to the animal, seeing it sent off for slaughter was far more difficult than she could stand.

There were also classes outside the farming and homemaking areas. My mother Grace Zerlaut was responsible for my life-long love of photography. She taught arts and crafts as well. One particular year, though, we studied entomology and took on butterflies, moths, and dragonflies. We captured these little insects and put them in killing jars. These glass fruit jars had a cotton ball soaked in chloroform in the bottom and a tight lid. After the insects died—beautiful orange and black Monarchs, pale green Luna moths with tissue-paper wings—we pinned them to Styrofoam inside a display box with a glass top, which my mother made for us. Then we labeled them with their scientific names.

Mother always put forth one hundred per cent effort when she was a leader; but as a young teenager, I did not always appreciate this—and one time, I was even embarrassed. To get an even wider range of insects, she made each of us little butterfly nets—and one for herself. She took us to a swampy area behind the home of Herbert and Rose Smith. She began chasing dragonflies and swooping her net. I was mortified then, but now it is one of my fondest memories of my mother, who proved she would do anything to help us in our endeavors.

Being part of the Sitka 4-H had its social side as well. We had annual Halloween and Christmas parties. Many of us also attended 4-H camp held at the Newaygo County Youth Camp at Hess Lake.

Chapter Twenty-four: The Post-War Years

* * *

Besides the closing of schools, other changes took place. In 1952, Dickinson Ave. was finally paved. Gone were the muddy ruts in the road. The general store closed for good in 1957 by owner Matt Glasen. Fourteen years later it was torn down. Nothing now remains of the store or its attachments—no sign of the creamery, post office, mill, and blacksmith shop exist.

In 1960, longtime resident, Mrs. Beth, then a widow, sold her farm and moved to Florida to be closer to her son Warren, who was in the space program. In her place came new owners, Ed and Ellie Dezinski. They brought with them musical talent they shared with the Sitka United Methodist Church for many years. Ed was a wonderful songwriter. He and his wife sang as he played the guitar.

Not all new neighbors, though, brought positive changes to Sitka. In 1958, my brother-in-law, who lived in Cedar Creek Township, sought a building permit. He was told he could buy cement blocks from anyone except The Liberty Cement Block Company in Muskegon, owned by Peter and Luella Corinti. Almost all townships and cities had banned the use of their cement blocks because they disintegrated from too much sand in their construction. (Later my brother, Allen Zerlaut, accepted cement blocks in lieu of payment from Mrs. Corinti. It wasn't long before they began to crumble.) The company closed and in 1960 the owners bought the farm formerly owned by the Clifford Holmes family in Sitka. This was the property originally settled by Holly Crawford just after the Civil War. For about ten years Luella also owned 150 acres of pasture land on Fitzgerald near Mystery Lake. The new owners called their home the "Liberty Farm".

There was never much "liberty" at the cement block company or the farm. Somehow Luella had reached an agreement allowing prisoners from the Muskegon County jail to receive an early parole if they agreed to work for her. She ran her business like a company store. At the cement block company the parolees lived on site in tiny cement block houses, about the size of a small camper trailer, for which they had to pay rent. They were also charged for food. When she closed the cement block company, she had two large cement block barracks built at the Liberty Farm next to the road, and took the parolees and her long time foreman, George Fredrickson, with her. Husband, Peter Corinti, never seemed to be in the picture, either at the cement block company, or at the farm.

When Luella appeared on the scene in Sitka, she was quite an unusual character. Even though she was a very large woman in a wheelchair, it did not stop her from doing anything she wanted. It was rumored she kept a gun under the blanket she always kept across her lap. She could drive a car, but would take along a passenger who would go into places for her to secure what she needed, such as eggs from my brother Allen's farm. What was unusual though, is she had the backseat taken out of the car so her Shetland pony could ride with her. She was also known to go around with a very nasty monkey.

Luella drove fear into those who worked for her and her arrival disrupted the relative peace of Sitka. For the first time, people began locking their doors at night and bringing the keys to the car inside the house. There was good reason for this caution. The men who lived at the Liberty Farm were all too familiar with crime and violence.

Shortly after the arrival of Luella, her foreman, and the parolees, there was a large upswing of crime in the area. The police were often called to the residence. Knives seemed to play a big role in their lives. One incident involved calling the police for help regarding a knife fight. When they arrived there was a lot of blood, but no victim in sight—and no one was talking.

My sister Arlene had her own confrontation with a knife. Some of the parolees had brought their families with them and lived in small houses, also built along 96th St. next to the barracks. One day during apple season

Chapter Twenty-four: The Post-War Years

my father and sister were finishing up after the apple pickers had left for the day. They were moving the big apple boxes—the empty ones to the rows that were to be picked the following day, and the full ones to the truck to be hauled to market. These large boxes, built in 1962 by Arlene and her husband, replaced the small apple crates. Each could hold eighteen and a half bushels of apples.

As Arlene rounded the corner, she saw someone duck behind an apple box. She approached and got off the tractor, when a boy about twelve came out from behind the box with a knife. By the time my dad saw what was happening and arrived on scene, my sister seemed to have it all under control. The boy had lowered the knife. After being interrogated by my father, he admitted that the bucket he was carrying was one Luella had given him to go steal apples.

It was getting late in the day and work needed to be finished, so it was not until early the next morning that my father decided to settle this business. He arrived at Luella's door only to be told by the housekeeper that she was still in bed. He pushed past her and went directly to her bedroom—where Luella sat, still in her nightgown. He proceeded to tell her in no uncertain terms that she needed to stop the thievery, get her people under control, and no one was ever to threaten his family again.

Their presence affected everyone in the area. Farmers could no longer leave their tractors in the fields overnight, or they would be vandalized. If leaving equipment in the orchard overnight, my father would take out the battery and drain the gas tank. That must have been quite an inconvenience.

The parolees at Liberty Farm were dealt with harshly by Luella. She ran her company store in such a way that by pay day, once she had subtracted their rent, the food they ate, and anything else she could think of, they often had little money left, or owed her! If by chance they had money, it is rumored she forced them to play cards with her and inevitably she won back any money they had left. If they gave her any trouble, she told them she would have them sent back to jail. In this way she had complete control over their lives. So it is no surprise that some tried to escape.

Myrna (Zerlaut) Brenner remembers a night when she was terribly frightened. A neighbor had come by to alert her parents that people were out searching for a man who had disappeared from the Liberty Farm. The neighbor wanted them to be aware this person could be hiding somewhere in one of their farm buildings. Despite the fact her parents were home, she and her sister Laura were so frightened they slept all night in their upstairs bedroom closet.

Mark Worthing also remembers a time, as a young teenager, when he became frightened. He and his cousin, Mac Zerlaut, were alone pruning trees for their grandfather, Harold Zerlaut, in the apple orchard near the church. When Harold had not returned at the appointed time, they sat down and listened to their radio. This is when they learned the police were looking for a man with a knife, who was last seen in an orchard in Sitka! They grabbed their pruners and climbed the highest apple tree they could find, and stayed until finally Harold came looking for them. He could not get to them sooner as the police had the roads blocked off. It was later learned the man with the knife had doubled back and was found hiding in a cornfield behind the Liberty farm, and was apprehended.

It was easy to blame all crime and maliciousness on the people from Liberty Farm. True, some really bad people lived there and were responsible for many problems. Others were people who just got trapped in the vicious circle Luella had designed to keep her workers from leaving, by making them unable to get out of her debt. They, too, became victims.

Chapter Twenty-five

The Milk Withholding Action

The National Farmers Organization (NFO) was organized in 1955. By the middle 1960s, a chapter in Newaygo County had been established. Its purpose was to combat low prices from food processors. In December 1966, more than 10,000 voting delegates attended the annual NFO convention in Milwaukee, Wisconsin. Representing the Newaygo County chapter were Allen Zerlaut, Mr. and Mrs. Tom Kempf, Mike Pell, Harold Zeldenrust, and Marve Westra. At this convention the board of directors of the NFO was given authorization to take steps towards a milk withholding action in hopes of raising the price to farmers by two cents a quart from the dairy processors. Members of twenty-five states agreed to participate.

Returning home the delegates met with other local members—Harvey Matthews, Ruth Beebe, Ken Stroven, George Stroven, Evert Deur, and George Shriver, Jr—to discuss the action. Allen Zerlaut, the county president of the NFO, said: 'No one should oppose this dynamic new approach. It is something farmers have always been told they should do. Now they can use NFO to reduce the size of the agricultural plant and bring supply in balance with demand.' (The Muskegon Chronicle, February 23, 1967). The action was set to begin March 16.

The decision to withhold milk was not a new one. Throughout the 1930's there were many disruptions by organized labor, but farm strikes also played an important role in shaping the price for products. State by state, the farmers banded together as a force to be reckoned with when determining what they would receive for payment from the dairy processing companies.

In Michigan, a nine day milk strike had been held in late March 1956. The farmers, who attempted to organize into a union-type group, picketed dairies and dumped milk. Threats and violence occurred frequently throughout the state. In Detroit, rocks, pipes, and sticks were used as weapons against non-striking farmers who attempted to deliver their milk to dairies. Milk trucks had to run blockades, often with police escorts. These escorts, plus a court order to stop picketing, brought the strike to an end. However, the leaders of the strike claimed victory as a price increase was won.

This earlier strike affected the area surrounding Sitka, as well. Basil Young, a descendent of Robert McKie, had a milk route in 1956. His daughter, Christine (Young) Parrish, remembers her father had an armed man riding with him during the strike. Luckily, he never felt he was put in danger, though he did run into men protesting. Several men were at the Bridgeton Bridge near the farm of Mr. Rose when he was on his way to the dairy processor, but they let him cross peacefully.

Throughout the strike of 1967, the Muskegon Chronicle recorded the news of the withholding action. Four days into the NFO milk strike, a million dollar law suit was filed by the Michigan Milk Producers Association (MMPA) against the national president of the NFO, Oren Lee Staley of Iowa, citing the use of force and threats to stop milk shipments. The Detroit dairies had received an anonymous pay-phone threat that milk had been tainted with arsenic. Gallons of shipments of milk were tested, but no contamination was found. One milk hauler near Imlay City had the front windows of his home broken by a dynamite explosion. Another explosion happened at the farm of a price negotiator for the MMPA, an opponent of the NFO. Milk truck haulers reported shots fired into their tankers.

Unlike other withholding actions, such as those involving grain and livestock where products could be held off the market for indefinite periods of time, the short shelf-life of milk posed a unique problem. What do to with the milk? Members of the NFO began dumping hundreds of thousands of gallons of milk. Many of the Newaygo members fed their milk to their pigs and other animals, but not all milk could be used, and

Chapter Twenty-five: The Milk Withholding Action

much of it was dumped. Not everyone, however, was dumping milk. There were those outside the NFO organization who were against the milk dumping, as were some of the members themselves. This caused friction between neighbors and friendships were strained as each farmer made hard choices.

Violence continued around the state and country, but the Newaygo County chapter frowned on violent actions. However, one particular fire in Sitka was investigated by police as suspicious. About 9:30 on the evening of March 23, Luella Corinti, known as the owner of the Liberty Farm, saw a vacant home on her property go up in flames. By the time the fire department arrived, the house was completely engulfed. Mrs. Corinti believed the fire was connected to the milk dumping action.

> She has been cooperating with the National farmers Organization, although not a member, in dumping the dairy output of her Liberty Dairy Farm, which milks 160 cows daily. Mrs. Corinti said she had lost an estimated $1200 through dumping milk and Thursday decided she would ship her milk. She said a group of farmers, realizing her financial plight, offered her $200 and she again withheld shipment. She was not prepared today to say whether the fire would have any bearing on her decision to continue dumping or resume shipping her milk. (The Muskegon Chronicle, March 14, 1967)

To keep her from sending her milk to the dairy processor, Allen Zerlaut bought Mrs. Corinti's milk. He transported the milk about a half mile to his farm in large tanks used to keep cherries cool during harvest season, and fed the milk to his pigs.

The cause of the fire remained undetermined. Harold Zeldenrust, vice-president of the NFO, released this statement the following day stressing they were trying to keep things peaceful. 'The demonstrations are being staged across the country to draw attention to the fact farmers are not getting enough money for their milk. We are stopping no vehicles. It's just a demonstration.' (The Muskegon Chronicle, March 25, 1967)

Michigan farmers were warned that they may face prosecution if they continued to cause pollution by dumping milk into streams. One tanker truck carrying 10,000 gallons could kill all the aquatic life in a stream. The fine for dumping in streams and rivers was $500.

By the thirteenth day of the action, some areas in the country were beginning to see success and had contracts for a two cent increase per quart. They also received the support of the Teamsters, the Meat Cutters Union, and the United Auto Workers.

As the milk withholding action began to wind down, the struggle for better prices continued by using a different method. Harold Zeldenrust stated that 'the farmers in Western Michigan will send 1,000 dairy cows to slaughterhouses in protest over current milk prices paid them... Mr. Zeldenrust, who owns 300 cows, said the NFO here is no longer dumping, but is continuing a partial withholding. He explained that as much as possible they are having their milk processed into butter and other byproducts and the rest is being sent to the market for bottling.' (The Muskegon Chronicle, April 1, 1967). Farmers pledged to send one cow each to market, thereby reducing the overall amount of milk processed.

Fifteen days into the action a temporary restraining order was issued by a US Federal Judge. Most believed the strike to be over. By the time the restraining order expired the government had negotiated terms with the NFO.

In December 1967 another NFO convention was held in Louisville, Kentucky. Alongside of executive members Allen Zerlaut and Harold Zeldenrust, delegates included Mr. and Mrs. Max Kempf, Junior Bayne, Roy Hillard and Art Snyder. Again, to improve prices for farmers, new actions were planned. This was called an all-commodity withholding action which began with plans to stop selling grain within forty days. They later planned to withhold everything from potatoes to asparagus. The NFO was asking non-members not to leave their present organizations, like the Farm Bureau, but to join in solidarity with their protests.

The success of these withholding actions can be debated. The many members who were part of the organization then have now passed on and the NFO in Newaygo County is not what it used to be. Nor is farming what it was then. The rural landscape is no longer dotted with small family farms. In their stead are mega-farms, which consider themselves business people more than farmers. The owners of these farms can negotiate better prices for themselves, leaving the small farmer without much of a voice. Today, these huge farms dwarf those of small family farmers, who just want to make a living like their ancestors did.

Chapter Twenty-six
Sitka Today

Only two of the original buildings remain in Sitka today. The Sitka Methodist Episcopal Church, on the corner of Dickinson Ave and 96th St., joined with the Evangelical United Brethren in 1968, at which time the church was renamed the Sitka United Methodist Church. Even though the front entrance to the church was later enclosed, the rest of the building looks much the same as it did when it was built in 1908. The over one hundred year old stained glass windows still reflect beautiful light on the sanctuary. The church bell is rung every Sunday morning as parishioners sit on the original pews waiting for service to begin. As a church, the people of Sitka church continue to fulfill its statement of purpose: 'Making God's presence felt throughout the community.' Their help to those in need in the community is well-known.

The Grange hall still stands and now belongs to the Sitka Community Club. For nearly three decades it fell into disuse. Animals had taken over and many repairs were needed inside and out. The building has been recently rescued and many renovations have taken place—new siding and windows, insulation, new furnace and wiring, and many other updates have made it once again a place for the community to gather.

Just west of the Sitka Hall the cement block barracks of the Liberty Farm remain in all their ugliness. Dark and foreboding, with missing roofs and windows, surrounded by brush and overgrown trees, they give off a haunted feeling. One wonders at all that took place within their walls during the twenty-five years Liberty Farm was in operation.

Luella Corinti's second husband Peter died in 1979, still unknown to the Sitka community. His obituary listed him as a resident of Grant with an occupation of road contractor. Just months before Luella died in 1984, she married her long-time foreman, George Fredrickson, fifteen years her junior. The property passed from her estate to William Fitzgerald and George Fredrickson. Within two years William had also passed on, and as sole owner, George sold the property to the current owner, Alice Kempf, and left the area.

Sadly, the ancestral home of my great-great-grandmother, Elizabeth Steiner Zerlaut, that feisty widow who braved the ocean with seven children in tow, was burned to the ground in 1974. The owner, Katie Zerlaut, was married to Elizabeth's grandson, Herman Zerlaut. Her grandson, Stan Bolt and wife, were renting the home at the time. All the belongings of a long-standing family in Sitka were destroyed. Gone were not only family photos, antiques, and mementoes, but also the World War II medals of Katie's son Laverne, and the Civil War uniform of Joseph A. Zerlaut.

The cause of the fire was arson, which makes it all the sadder. This fire was one of two set that day. The second home, just two miles away, belonged to the family of Jim Zacharias. No one was home at either location. Nothing much was salvageable from either fire. Robbery appeared to be the motive. Just three years later the barn on the same Zerlaut farm, then owned by Allen Zerlaut, burned to the ground, along with 2500 bales of hay. This ended over one hundred years' existence of this homestead. The property is still in the Zerlaut family, now belonging to Allen's daughter, Laura Zerlaut.

The orchards of Harold Zerlaut on the corner of the Sitka crossroads, no longer belong to the Zerlaut family. The trees still exist, but after many years of neglect they have declined and cease to be productive. After the passing of Harold, and later his son and wife, Allen and Marjorie Zerlaut, much of the Zerlaut property was divided and sold.

This was true of many of the farms in the area. People died, or could not make it financially farming, and their land was sold and the family left the area. Some farms were split into smaller acreages. From the original settlers of Sitka, four families of their descendants still farm to some extent. They are the families of the Kempfs, Jibsons, Matthews, and Zerlauts.

Epilogue

When I look back on the changes that have taken place during my lifetime, they are quite amazing; but they are nothing in comparison to the vast transformations that happened in my father's generation. Born in 1899, he grew up walking behind a horse with a plow, and lived to sit in front of his TV set watching a man land on the moon. Who could have predicted that?

Things we take for granted now, made huge changes in the lives of the people of Sitka. The coming of age of the automobile and steam engines made work and travel much easier. When growing up my father would sometimes get out the old horse drawn wagon and sleigh. It seemed impossible to me then that anyone would use such things on a daily basis.

Though the steam engine originally owned by J. Albert Ruggles was no longer used in my childhood, it still made a mighty impression on me. Mr. Ruggles was a man who overcame difficult physical handicaps to make a living. When he was a year old, he was afflicted with infantile paralysis. For his entire life he was unable to walk without crutches, but still managed his farm and ran heavy equipment. He bought the steam engine thresher in 1917. With his threshing crew, he worked farm to farm during the harvest season. Large mid-day meals were prepared for the threshers at each farm. By the time I was about five, the current owners would take the thresher out for a spin now and then. I could hear it coming down the road as the whistle blew, and ran for cover—which usually meant hiding behind the sofa in the living room. Even then, I could not resist raising my head to peek out the window to watch this huge relic go by.

Early in the 1900s many began moving from just having bare necessities, to procuring more luxury items, which were dutifully reported in the Sitka News. "Adam Freudenstein got a new Victrola." "Miss Loretta Rummelt is the proud owner of a new piano." "Fred Matthews put in a telephone this week." Telephones were on a party line system, which proved to be a boon for gossip. These party lines were in place until the mid-1970s. One neighborhood woman was so well known for listening in on the phone calls of her neighbors that they often involved her in their conversations. Other times they would "plant" untrue gossip and wait to see how fast it would travel through the community. Not long.

The most excitement came when the community finally got electricity. In March 1936 a very large crowd met at the Sitka Hall in order to sign electrical contracts. They had high hopes that it would not take long for electricity to reach them, but by July they were still waiting. In November it was reported that it was getting closer so they just needed to have more patience. Finally, in December, people got their long awaited electricity and decided to have a celebration. "The party at the Sitka hall given by the Grange last Saturday night for the celebration of the new electric line was very well attended and all enjoyed a fine program, dancing and supper." (Fremont Times Indicator, January 14, 1937)

By the time the electricity arrived, I can understand the excitement they must have felt. One of the big holdups had been the winter weather. The year 1936 brought enormous snowstorms. Schools were closed for extended periods. Due to huge drifts, one teacher was unable to get back to her own home for three weeks. Mail was undeliverable. Even deer died due to starvation.

Besides all the changes that took place, I am left with some lasting impressions of the people of Sitka. Education was very important to them. One of the very first things they did was erect two schools. They also believed in education for the adults, through programs at Grange Hall meetings and various other activities. They were constantly learning.

They were very social people who frequently gathered to share a meal—the good old chicken dinner—listen to music, and to dance. They were hard working people who usually had completed a hard day's work before enjoying such entertainment.

They were there to help each other when illness or tragedy struck. Time and time again I read about them helping each other, such as helping to rebuild a barn that was destroyed, or gathering clothing for a family in need.

They were always there to support the troops during the wars, whether it was through sending care packages, or volunteering to do Red Cross work.

When there was work to be done, they pitched in and did it. They had to constantly do repair work on the roads, and made sure the schools, hall, and church had an ample supply of firewood.

I "met" people through this journey that I will never forget. The strength of Laura Matthews who fought to have a church in Sitka, is an example of faith and perseverance, even when life dealt her deadly lows.

The Crawford family I will remember as an example of how to support your community. They provided the land for the Grange Hall. They held positions of postmaster, pathmaster, school teachers, Sunday school teachers, and even band director.

Then there were the men who went off to fight in the Civil War, though many had just barely arrived in this country, and the women and children left behind in the wilderness who had to carry on, who showed so much courage. And who could forget John Kempf, who tried to re-enlist when he was just days from dying?

These forward looking people, whose strengths have been passed down generation to generation, make me proud to say, I am a child of Sitka.

Appendices

Teachers of Kempf School
Sheridan Township, District #4

Guy Crawford, born in Sheridan Twp., November 27, 1876, went to school in the frame building located where the brick school stood in later years. The following are teachers he remembered from the early years of Kempf School.

Alfred Anderson	David Crawford	Bert Miler
Tillie Aslakson	John Chester Crawford	Jessie Naye
Sadie Baker	Lillie Evans	Swell Rodgers
Helen Bean	Eva Fry	Jon Winters
Ida Bennett	Myra Gordon	

The following list of teachers is taken from the Intermediate School District records of Newaygo County for 1901-1926.

(1901-1903)	Chauncey Miller
(1903-1904)	Maude L. Wilcox, Katie Clark
(1906-1907)	Birdie Miller
(1907-1909)	Maude L. Wilcox
(1909-1910)	Eva B. Wile
(1910-1911)	Seane Berry, Edwin E. Warren
(1911-1913)	S. S. Rogers, Harry L. Spooner
(1913-1915)	Birdie B. Miller
(1915-1917)	Carrie Ruprecht
(1917-1918)	Christina Kempf

(1918-1919)   Christina (Kempf) Parisian
(1919-1921)   Milissa Wilcox
(1921-1922)   Cecil Wright
(1922-1923)   Lotus Wallace Stemple
(1923-1924)   Treasure (Dunklee) Morse,
(1924-1925)   Unknown
(1925-1926)   Lena Griswold

Former students remember teachers:

Jeanette Anderson, Mrs. Caseltine, Mrs. Dunning, Hildar Freudenstein, Mrs. Goyings, Elizabeth Hansen, Mrs. Smith, Mrs. Southland, and Martha Vile.

Appendices

Students of Kempf School (1901-1902)

Frank Crevier	Archibald Malett	Daniel Schank
Eva Dubrey	Edward Malett	George Schank
Bertha Everhart	Estella Malett	Freddie Young
Freeman Kempf	Lilly Malett	Harold Young
Gilbert Kempf	George Matthews	Herman Zerlaut
Harold Kempf	Elvin McCormick	Martin Zerlaut
Lilly M. Kempf	Eva Nelson	
Raymond Kempf	Elna Rainouard	
Lawrence Lyon	George Rainouard	
Lester Lyon	Charles Reed	
Tresse Lyon	Earnest Reed	
Alvin Maelison	George Reed	
Louise Maelison	Albert Resterhouse	
Roy Maelison	Glen Ruggles	
Willie Maelison	Helen Ruggles	

Students of Kempf School (1911-1912)

Sylva Buck	Arthur Kempf	Willie Rummelt
Veda Buck	Ernest Kempf	Benny Sneller
Laura Crawford	Harold Kempf	Willie Sneller
Russell Crawford	Luella Kempf	Malissa Wilcox
Della Coutchie	Mabel Kempf	Mae Wilson
Eugene Coutchie	Neva Kempf	Beatrice Young
Illa Coutchie	Archibald Malett	Harry Young
Laura Coutchie	Harry Nash	Johnnie Young
Sidney Coutchie	Ruth Nash	Joseph Young
Velora Coutchie	Carl Rummelt	Lillie Young
Laura Crawford	Loretta Rummelt	Louie Young
Russell Crawford	Martin Rummelt	Paul Young

Appendices

Students of Kempf School (1924-1925)

Ferdinand Bissen	Evelyn Miller	Alma Rummelt
Max Buck	Howard Miller	Loretta Rummelt
Veda Buck	Robert Miller	Eugene Rhowmine
Dorothy Coutchie	Algot Murray	Henry Sherman
Eugene Coutchie	Beatrice Murray	James Start
Napolean Coutchie	June Murray	Bert Vischer
Arnold Hagen	Orval Murray	John Vischer
Charlie Hagen	Rozella Murray	Pearl Vischer
Harvey Hagen	Frankie Nash	Lucille Young
Joseph Hagen	Holly Nash	Paul Young
Marian Kempf	Rosa Nash	Violet Young
Maxwell Kempf	Charles Nelson	Laverne Zerlaut
Charles Matthews	Lorena Nelson	Leona Zerlaut
Harvey Matthews	Orabell Nelson	Leonard Zerlaut
Margaret Matthews	Paul Nelson	Maxine Zerlaut
Vivian Matthews	Iva Ruggles	Maynard Zerlaut
Barbara McDonald	Thelma Ruggles	

Teachers of Jibson School
Bridgeton Township, District #3

(1883) Anna Vanderbelt

The following list of teachers is taken from the Intermediate School District records of Newaygo County for 1901-1926.

(1901-1902)	Helen Bean
(1902-1903)	Maggie Roysdton
(1903-1904)	Hazel Ketchum
(1904-1905)	Hattie Sage, Ellis Armantrout, Bertha Sischo
(1905-1906)	Bertha Smith
(1906-1907)	Bertha Frye
(1907- 1908)	Fausta Starn
(1908-1909)	Mattie E. Warren
(1909-1910)	Anna Lehman
(1910-1911)	Clara Mead, Carrie Ruprecht
(1911-1913)	Stasia Donahue
(1913-1914)	Merta Church, Anna Vanderbelt
(1914-1916)	Stasia Donahue
(1916-1917)	Gladys Parker
(1917-1918)	Irma Miller
(1918-1919)	Neva Zerlaut
(1919-1920)	Pearl McQueen, Fausta Starn
(1920-1922)	Mary Ruprhect

(1922-1923)   Marion Jibson

(1923-1924)   Neva (Zerlaut) Chrystler

After 1926 from various records, the following teachers taught at Jibson School:

(1928-1929)   Mrs. Hunt

(1937-1939)   Hildar Anderson

(1940-1941)   Jeanette Anderson

(1945-1954)   Stasia (Donahue) Ruprecht

(1954-1957)   Ella Mae Powles

(1957-1962)   Elizabeth Hansen

(1962-1966)   Mrs. Miller

(1966-1967)   Judy Somers

Students of Jibson School (1901-1902)

Anna Anderson	Katie Kempf	Millie Ruprecht
Christina Anderson	Werner Kempf	Russell Ruprecht
Emma Anderson	Anna Lehman	Warren Ruprecht
Lena Bucher	Christina Lehman	Blanche Squires
Mytle Bucher	Jane Lehman	Lela Squires
Frank Carr	Julia Lehman	Neva Thomson
Grace Carr	Paul Lehman	Flossie Winget
Leslie Carr	Reka Lehman	
Clara Freudenstein	Rosa Lehman	
Martin Freudenstein	Paul Lehman	
Mary Jibson	Louis Ruprecht	

Students of Jibson School (1911-1912)

Raymond Freudenstein	Marion Jibson	Anna McKie
Dee Gardenour	Martin Jibson	Stella McKie
Don Gardenour	Mary Jibson	L. B. Murrey
Letha Gardenour	Richard Jibson	Russell Ruprecht
Roy Gardenour	Elsie Kempf	Leo Ruggles
Orville Garedenour	Lenroa Kempf	Frank Thill
Ester Halverson	Werner Kempf	John Thill
Pearl Huntoon	Amelia Lehman	Goldie Wilde
Marion Huntoon	Frederica Lehman	Grover Wilde
Montie Huntoon	Julia Lehman	Harold Zerlaut
Roy Huntoon	Oscar Lehman	Lavina Zerlaut
Dorothy Jibson	Paul Lehman	Neva Zerlaut

Students of Jibson School (1924-1925)

Clarence Baker	Howard Jibson	Edna Nieusma
Gilbert Crampton	Lloyd Jibson	Lillian Nieusma
Raymond Freudenstein	Richard Jibson	Bernice Sorenson
Gerald Hanson	Ellwood Kempf	Clarence Sorenson
Arthur Haske	Lyle Kempf	Edwin Sorenson
Gerritt Haske	Verne Kempf	Raymond Smith
Laura Jibson	Marie Nieusma	

Appendices

Sitka Methodist Episcopal Church Subscription Document of 1908

The following are the names of those who signed the subscription promising funds to support the building of the Sitka Episcopal Methodist Church. Names are as they appeared on the document.

Alfred Anderson	Ole Hanson	D. N. Markley
John Anderson (Fremont)	Gladis Huntoon	Fred Matthews
John Anderson (Holton)	Willard Huntoon	Mrs. Fred Matthews
Peter Anderson	William Huntoon	Henry Matthews
Dr. B. F. Black	John Jibson	Amza Morrison
C. L. Boyd	Martin Jibosn	Frank Nash
Rev. W. H. H. Bunch	Peter Jibson	John Nash
Mrs. William Carr	Sadie Jibson	A. S. Nelson
Ezra Cady	Alvin Johnson	Henry O'Connor
George Crawford	Clarence Johnson	Mrs. Henry O'Connor
Guy Crawford	Gilbert Kempf	Herbert O'Connor
H. W. Crawford	Gustave Kempf	A. C. Palmer
John Crawford	Herald Kempf	B. F. Palmer
Lynn Crawford	Robert Kempf	Ralph Palmer
P. H. Crawford	W. A. Kempton	William Palmer
Russel Crawford	Anna Lehman	Carrie Racey
Vernon & Francis Crawford	Paul Lehmann	Clyde Ruggles
	Lizzie Moon	Glen Ruggles
William Crystler	Martin Moon	Henry Ruggles
Mary Fergueson	L. L. White	Raymond Young

Louis Ruprecht   James Whiteside   William Young
Louis Ryerson   Mr. Wooden   Henry E. Zerlaut
Mattie Warren   Fosta Storms   Herman Zerlaut
John Weiler   Fred Young   J. A. Zerlaut
James Whaley   John Young   Martin Zerlaut
B. White

Other donations:
Cash from Fremont   Boven & Co.
Church Extension Society   Holton Brick Co.
Collection from L. A. Society   O'Conner Bros.

General Collection:
Mrs. A. J. Nash: 110 bricks
Bert Nelson: 9 sacks of plaster
Martin Jibson: 9 bunches shingles, 1000 lath

Total Value: $2114.59

Members of the Ladies Aid Society 1908

Bertha Crawford	Effie Jibson	Bertha White
Luella Crawford	Sadie Jibson	Mamie Young
Mae Crawford	Laura Markley	Lola Zerlaut
Anna Freudenstien	Laura Matthews	Mary Zerlaut
Clara Hanson	Helen Ruggles	

Bibliography

Abbot, Ethelyn Thersa. Michigan History Stories for Boys and Girls. Hillsdale School Supply Company, 1947.

Alexander, Jeff. The Muskegon, The majesty and Tragedy of Michigan's Rarest River. Michigan State University Press, 2006

Catton, Bruce. Michigan: A Bicentennial History. New York: W. W. Norton and Company Inc., 1976

Chisholm, John A. "The Chisholm Trail". Muskegon Chronicle. Sept. 12, 1970

Clifton, James et al. The Ottawa, Patawatomi and Ojibway of Michigan. Grand Rapids: The Michigan Indian Press. Grand Rapids Inter-Tribal Council, 1986

Dix, Edwin Asa. Champlain, The Founders of New France. New York: d. Appleton and Company, 1903

Edward, Lissa, "Madame La Framboise Harbour View Inn Preserves the Story of a 19th Century French/Indian Mackinac Island Entrepreneur" at http://mynorth.com/2015/05/madame-la-framboise-harbour-view-in-preserves-the-story-of- (accessed Apr. 1, 2016)

Evans, Martha. "Joseph Troutier, 'Trukee" First Fur Trader on Muskegon River". Unpublished document, no date available, available at Fremont Area District Library.

Frazier, Jean. Kah-wam-da-meh (We See Each Other). Grand Ledge, Michigan: The Herman E. Cameron Memorial Foundation. 1988

Goss, Dwight. "Indians of Grand River Valley Michigan." L'Anse, Michigan: Mike Joki, no date.

Herrington, Walter Stewart. The Martyrs of New France. Toronto: William Briggs, 1909

Holly W. Crawford. Obituary. Fremont Times Nov. 20, 1913.

Johnson, Ida Amanda. The Michigan Fur Trade. Lansing Historical

Commission, 1919.

Kempf, Warner. Notes on the history of the Kempf family, compiled 1969.

King, Susan. Letters Home. Terry Wantz Historical Research Center, 2013.

Kubiak, William J. Great Lakes Indians. Grand Rapids, Michigan: Baker Books, A Division of Baker House Co., 1970

Lewis Crawford. Obituary. Fremont Times Indicator Dec. 18, 1930

Lewis J Crawford. Obituary. "Grant Veteran Mustered Out". The Newaygo Republican Dec. 18, 1930, available at The Fremont Historical Center.

Matthews, Laura. "A Brief Review of the Rise and Struggles and Success of the Methodist Episcopal Church of Holton and Sitka from 1872-1917" presented at Sitka March 12 1917. Unpublished.

Meier, Michael T. "Civil War Draft Records: Exemptions and Enrollments". Winter 1994, Vol. 26, No.4. at http://www.archives.gov/publications/prologue/1994/winter/civil-war-draft-rcords.html (accessed July 7, 2016)

Samuel Crawford. Civil War Soldier Records and Profiles, 1861-1865. http://search.ancestry.com/gibin/see.dll?_phsrc=Gfs620&_phstart=successSource&useP. (accessed Aug. 12, 2016)

Spooner, Harry L. "Curious Cross Is Local Find", News-Indicator-Vol. XLX, No 27, (Feb. 22, 1923), available at Fremont Historical Center.

Spooner, Harry L. "Indians of Oceana," Michigan History Magazine, Vol. XV, 1931

The Civil War in the East. "3rd Michigan" at http://civilwarintheeast.com/us-regiments-batteries/michigan/3rd-michigan/ (accessed July 15, 2016)

Thwaites, Reubin Gold. Father Marquette. New York: Dr. D. Appleton and Company, 1910.

Troutier, Antoine. U. S., Civil War Soldier Records and Profiles, 1861-1865 at http://search.ancestry.com/search/collections/civilwar_histdatasys/745783/ (accessed July 7, 2016)

Zehrlaut, Alwin. 'Elizabeth Steiner Zerlaut.' Letter from Alwin Zehrlaut, Kempten, Gerberstasse to Szabo family. Copy in possession of author.

Zehrlaut, Alwin. 'Elizabeth Steiner Zerlaut.' Letter from Alwin Zehrlaut, Kempten, Gerberstasse to Walter Zerlaut, Apr. 24, 1959. Copy in possession of author.

Zerlaut, Herman. Notes for a presentation to Sitka Grange 1912 on the topic of Joseph Zerlaut's Civil War service.

Zerlaut, Walter. "John 'Nick" Kempf. 3rd Michigan Infantry, Civil War 1861-1864"complied from "The History of Newaygo County, Michigan Civil War Veterans, July 1984" and other sources. Unpublished.

Zerlaut, Walter."Joseph A. Zerlaut. 6th Michigan Calvary, 1862-1865". Compiled from "The History of Newaygo County, Michigan Civil War Veterans July 1984" and other sources. (Aug. 1985) Unpublished.

Unattributed Sources

"1918 Spanish Flu Pandemic" at http://history1900s.about.com/od/1910s/p/spanishflu.htm (accessed Jan. 18, 2011)

"3rd Michigan Volunteer Infantry Regiment" at http://en.wikipedia.org/wiki/3rd_Michigan_Volunteer_Infantry_Regiment (accessed July 15, 2016)

"A History of the Sitka, Michigan Community and Its Early Pioneers". No author. Published by the Sitka Community Club as a community service. 1970.

"A Pictorial Record of the Muskegon Lumbering Era" North Muskegon Historical Committee, 1976.

"About RBM Ministries!" at http://www.rbmminitries.org/aboutus.php (accessed July 31, 2017

"Alethea Utter," Obituary. Fremont Times Indicator July 18, 2001.

"American Farm Bureau Federation" at https://en.wikipedia.org/wiki/

American_Farm_Bureau_Federation" (accessed Oct. 16, 2017)

"An Interactive Jibson Family History" at http://www.geocities.com/jibsond/jhistory.htm?200518

"Anti-Saloon League" at https://britannica.com/topic/Anti-Saloon-League (accessed Aug. 15, 2017)

"Ardath F. Enszer," Oibtuary. Kroeze-Wolffis Funeral Home, Inc. at http://www.kroeze-wolffis.com/notices/Adath-Enzeeeer (accessed Aug. 3, 2017)

"Battle of the Bulge" at https://en.wikipedia.org/wiki/Battle_of_the_Bulge (accessed Dec. 01, 2017)

"Buckland Mills Battle" at http://www.hmdb.org/marker.asp?marker=19785 (accessed Dec. 8, 2010)

"Descendants of Sabrina Storms" at http://freepages.genealogy.rootsweb.ancestry.com?~storms1?Sabrina.htm (accessed March 29, 2016

"Diphtheria" at https://en.wiipedia.org/wiki/Diptheria

"Epworth League" at https://en.wikipedia.org/wiki/Epworth_League (accessed July 24, 2017)

"Erie Canal" at http://en.wikipedia.org/w/index.php?title=Erie_Canal (accessed March 30, 2016

"Fire levels two Sitka homes," Fremont Times Indicator, 1974

"Fred Matthews," Obituary. Fremont Times Indicator November 27, 1918.

"Great Depression in the United States" at https://en.wikipedia.org/wiki/Great_Depression_in_the_Untied_States (accessed Oct. 16, 2017)

"Holly W. Crawford," Obituary. Fremont Times Nov. 20, 1913.

"Holly W. Crawford. June 24, 1830-Nov. 9, 1913". No author. No date. On File with Fremont Historical Center.

"Homestead Act" at http://www.answers.com/topic/homestead-act (accessed Jan. 22, 2011)

"Indian Removal Act" at https://en.wikipedia.org/wiki/Indian_removal

(accessed June 9, 2016)

"J. Albert Ruggles," Obituary. Fremont Times Indicator Nov. 5, 1953.

"James W. Trumbull" at http://mv.ancestry.com (accessed Feb. 23, 2016).

"Jibson Family" at http://migenweb.org/newaygo/jivson.html

"John Jacob Astor and the Fur Trade: Testing the Role of Government". Folsom, Burton W. at http://fee.org/articles/john-jacob-astor-and-the-fur-trade-testing-the-role-of-goverment/ (accessed Apr. 1, 2016)

"John Jacob Astor" at https://en.wikipedia.org/w/index.php?title=John=Jacob=Astor (accessed Apr. 1, 2016)

"Joseph Bailly" at https://en.wikipedia.org/wiki/Joseph_Bailly (accessed Apr. 1, 2016)

"Living History: Battle of the Bulge, Courtesy of U. S. Army Center of Military History" at https:www.army.mil/both/ (accessed Dec. 12, 2017)

"Logging in Muskegon-The Ryerson Family" at http://rootsweb.ancestry.com/~mimuskeg/Ryerson.html (accessed June 6, 2016)

"Lookback: 1891 fire devastates Muskegon's Pine Street downtown business district". LeMieux, Dave. Muskegon Chronicle at http://blog.mlive.com/chronicle/news_impact/print.html?entry=/2012/05/lookback_1891_f (accessed Aug. 20, 2016)

"Luxembourg American Cemetery and Memorial" at https:en.wikipedia.org/wiki/Luxembourg_American_Cemetery_and_Memorial (accessed Nov. 29, 2017)

"Madame LaFramboise" at http://www.lowellmuseum.org/?pate_id=3664 (accessed Apr. 1, 2016)

"Magdelaine Laframboise" at https://en.wikipedia.org/wiki/Magdelaine_Laframboise (accessed Apr. 1, 2016)

"Michigan Fever, part 1" at http://geo.msu.edu/extra/geogmich/michigan_fever.html (accessed March 3, 2016)

"Michigan Territory" at https://en.wikipedia.org/w/index.

Bibliography

php?title=Michigan_Territory (accessed March 3, 2016)

"Mortgage. Joseph A. Zerlaut to Elizabeth Zerlaut," October 22, 1867. Liber 3 Mortgages, Page 251. Newaygo County.

"Muskegon County Early Days" at http://www.rootsweb.ancestry.coom/~mimuskeg/earlyda.html (accessed Aug. 8, 2016)

"Narzis Steiner," Obituary. Muskegon Chronicle Feb. 3, 1902.

"National Farmers Organization" at https://en.wikipedia.org/National_Farmers_Organization (accessed January 18, 2018)

"Native American Netroots" at http://nativeamericannetroots.net/diary/352 (assessed Dec. 6, 2017)

"Notes from Michigan Volunteers". John 'Nick" Kempf. Posted by Jake Stroven at http://mv.ancestry.com/viewer/49088a48-416c-407a-9b26-2blb63790ff2/2006915/-1359. (accessed Feb. 2, 2016)

"Obituary Daily Inter Ocean, Chicago, Illinois 7, Sep 1887", Martin Ryerson, Posted by ktolliver8864 Nov. 11, 2015 at http://mv.ancestry.com/viewer/ba0a341d-57e7-4031-a880-519e094aa360/16848446/19290 (accessed March 24, 2016)

"Pertussis" at http://en.wikipedia.org/wiki/Pertussis (accessed Aug. 20, 2016)

"Scarlet Fever" at https://en.wikipedia.org/wiki/Scarlet_fever

"Spanish Flu Pandemic Begins: March 1918" at Fold 3.com by Ancestry (accessed March 2, 2015)

"The Army Nurse Corps" at https://history.army.mil/books/wwii/72-14/72-14.HTM (accessed Oct. 13, 2017)

"The Early Years of Newaygo Co., Part I". Wantz, Terry E. Fremont Times Indicator. October 21, 1998

"The Early Years of Newaygo Co., Part II". Wantz, Terry E. Fremont Times Indicator. October 28, 1998

"The Homestead Act of 1862" at http://www.time-passages.com/homestead-act.html (accessed January 22, 2011)

"The Hugh Brady Letters and the Removal of the Potawatomis" at http://www.michiganletters.org/ (April 1, 2016)

"The New York Milk Strikes" at http://www.themilkhouse.org/?tag=1930s-strike (accessed January 18, 2018)

"The Tree that Never Dies, Oral History of the Michigan Indians", edited by Pamela J. Dobson, Grand Rapids, Michigan: Grand Rapids Public Library, 1978

"Treaty of Washington (1836)" at http://en.wikipedia.org/w/index.php?title=Treaty_of_Washington_(1836) (accessed March 3, 2016)

"Typhoid Fever" at http://en.wikipedia.org/wiki/Thypoid_fever

"U.S. Coffee Rationing in World War II" at https://www.coffeecrossroads.com/coffee-history/u-s-coffee-rationing-in-world-war-ii (accessed Nov. 20, 2017)

"Was Pioneer of Newaygo County". Fred Matthews. Obituary, Fremont Times Nov. 27. 1918.

"Women's Army Corps" at https://en.wikipedia.org/wiki/Women%27s_Army_Corps (accessed Nov. 28, 2017)

www.ingramcontent.com/pod-product-compliance
Lightning Source LLC
Chambersburg PA
CBHW052140070526
44585CB00017B/1910